CAUGHT FALLING

THE CONFLUENCE OF CONTACT IMPROVISATION, NANCY STARK SMITH, AND OTHER MOVING IDEAS

WRITTEN AND CONCEIVED BY
DAVID KOTEEN AND **NANCY STARK SMITH**

BACKWORDS BY **STEVE PAXTON**

CAUGHT FALLING

THE CONFLUENCE OF CONTACT IMPROVISATION, NANCY STARK SMITH, AND OTHER MOVING IDEAS

WRITTEN AND CONCEIVED BY

DAVID KOTEEN AND **NANCY STARK SMITH**

BACKWORDS BY **STEVE PAXTON**

photo: Roger Kose

Caught Falling: The confluence of Contact Improvisation, Nancy Stark Smith, and other moving ideas.

Design concept: David Koteen, Nancy Stark Smith
Book designers: Dave Snider, Lila Hurwitz (Ibirdesign), Joel Southern
Consulting editors: Norah Zuniga Shaw, David Gere
Proofreading: Jamie Nan Thaman
Printing and binding: Marcus Printing, Holyoke, MA

Front cover photo by Uldis Ohaks of Nancy performing with ReUnion at the San Francisco Museum of Art, San Francisco, California, 1976. (Clyfford Still painting in the background.)

"Hieroglyphs" throughout book by Nancy Stark Smith.

Photo/Image credits are on page 108.

Library of Congress Cataloging-in-Publication Data: (in process)

ISBN: 0-937645-09-5

Manufactured in the United States of America

Distributed by:
Contact Editions, P.O. Box 603, Northampton, MA 01061; (413) 586-1181
www.contactcollaborations.com - info@contactquarterly.com

table of contents

acknowledgments

When the making of a book spans fourteen years from inception to completion, many thanks accumulate. Some that can be remembered and acknowledged, others that remain invisible.

Big thanks to all the designers of this book: Joel Southern got us going, Lila Hurwitz (lbirdesign) brought us through the wild midzones, Dave Snider took us home.

Editorial support has been essential. David Gere read through early manuscripts and gave significant notes and direction. Norah Zuniga Shaw, a late blessing to the project (thanks, D. Gere!), plunged into the bookmaking process in its last stages with great energy, phenomenal editorial skill, and crucial help in guiding the book to completion.

Constructive feedback (holding no punches) from several individuals—Sally Nash, Simone Forti, Lisa Nelson, Beverly Sky, and Lila Hurwitz—has been invaluable in keeping spirits up while sharpening the blade of incisive vision and editing.

The Life Stories story: Following the surprising suggestion of trusted consultant, writer, and scholar David Gere that this book needed my "autobiography," I took on the daunting task with a score: to write for one hour per decade. I more or less (mostly less) kept to the score—scanning the decades and retrieving stand-alone "life stories." Later, Norah, DK, and I excerpted and edited the extensive material into the bite-size units you'll find in spheres throughout *Caught Falling.*

In the making and producing of this book, many thanks go to the *Contact Quarterly*/Contact Editions office and staff for facilities and support; to Simone Forti for repeated passes through the book, offering questions, curiosity, critiques, and encouragement; to Felice Wolfzahn for production assistance; to Jamie Thaman for fast, smart, detailed proofreading; to cousin Liz Schwartz Storch for emergency posting of family photos; to Gionatan Surrenti for feedback on early Underscore materials; to Bright Crosswell and Susan Jackson for astrological insight; to Lila Hurwitz for hanging in there with us for several years, giving comprehensive feedback along with excellent design work; to Steve Clorfeine for housing early interviews in his NYC apartment; to the Koteen boys for DNA therapy; to Sy Safransky and *The Sun* magazine for getting this whole thing rolling by welcoming the initial interview; and to Dave Snider for precise, patient, omnidirectional design work and commitment to the book's completion.

Wonder-full thanks to Sally Nash and her Workspace for Choreographers in Sperryville, Virginia, for the gift of space and time—two residencies at this inspiring facility with cabin and studio at the edge of the Shenandoah State Forest, along with Sally's strong, artistic suggestions and insistence that we go for our highest vision.

Thanks to several people for their kindness in housing our book retreats—on Vashon Island, Washington (Joan and Jon Hanna; Dana Illu and Catherine Johnson); in Western Mass. (Carolyn Shakti Sadeh); in Colorado (Rancho Vargas and the Pirates); in Eugene, Oregon (Fox Hollowland).

Thanks to sisters Susan Berenzweig and Ellen Koteen for taking care of us when we were young and for whole life support.

Thanks, Steve, for writing the Backwords! And Christie Svane for your inspiring birthday poem. And to family, friends, and colleagues who contributed "talk bubbles," as well as dear friend Judi Peavey for her loving letter of memories.

Photographers of dance—where would we be without them?—are always being asked to contribute their photos for little or no compensation, and this book is no exception. Bill Arnold, whose photos fill this book with his unique visual perspective, has been extremely generous with his images over the past three decades for *CQ* magazine and many book projects. Thanks also to Stephen Petegorsky, Uldis Ohaks, Ted Pushinsky, and others for regular use of their wonderful early photos of CI.

Other inspirations: We'd especially like to acknowledge Remy Charlip—dancer and visual artist—for his delightful children's book *Thirteen,* which provided the initial inspiration for the "windshields" in which several concurrent "stories" develop over the course of the book. And Cynthia Novack for the passion and integrity with which she researched and wrote her ethnography, *Sharing the Dance: Contact Improvisation and American Culture,* doing much to promote depth, intelligence, and humanity in the understanding of the dance form.

Mike Vargas for his love, support, art, music, and life.

And finally, special thanks to several incidental angels for their infusion of spirit when we needed it most.

Thank you all.
David and Nancy

This book is dedicated to probing life's mysteries through movement, and to the people whose work that is.

NSS

To self-liberation
& Simultaneous liberation of others
Which is both sides
Of contact improv

DK

photo: Roger Kose

prologue

Nancy and I have been working on this book, *Caught Falling*, on and off, in fits and starts, since 1994. It has truly been an engagement of two Aquarian, writer-type Contact Improvisers. Fun, research, and exploration; very challenging, always moving. A slow long-distance dance.

Caught Falling is about Nancy's life, about Contact Improvisation, about our mutual devotion to this endlessly delightful art-sport. We've generated volumes of material, edited and reedited, deleted, replaced, sought counsel, laughed at our complicated musings. How like a river, the book caught and swept us up in its current. Who knew where it would take us? What it would be?

Since the beginning of the project, my intention with *Caught* was to further disseminate information about CI, with Nancy as the medium: How she has unhesitatingly taken on major roles as Contact archivist, continuous editor of *Contact Quarterly*, initiator of CI25, and on and on. How she has wandered the globe like some peripatetic diva, embodying the spirit of Contact in her teaching, writing, performing, workshops, dance—life.

Take a look at *Caught Falling;* make contact with it; jam awhile...enjoy the ride!

David Koteen
2008

photo: Bruce Newhouse

David Koteen in *Onselfoffing*, Eugene, OR, 1991.

introduction

HE MADE ME DO IT

Caught Falling is a book about dancing and living made by two long-term practitioners of Contact Improvisation (CI), for whom that work has been central and inspiring. The book began as a simple interview about Contact Improvisation (CI) for *The Sun* magazine. Would you? David asked, wanting to introduce that grassroots, literary community to CI. He was eager. I said, Sure.

We started with a phone interview, which, having been transcribed by an unsuspecting, uninitiated woman-on-the-street whom DK found to do the job, produced a flow of amusing what-she-could-make-out approximations of what we were saying: "Contact Improvisation" became "contacting problemization," "contact and proposition," "contact probovision," and "contact of conversation," and a sentence that had originally ended with "...called Contact Improvisation" became one ending with "...cold, hot tech provivision."

After that first interview failed to produce the lucid nuggets of truth about CI we were looking for, DK invented a form I took to immediately. He sent me ten typewritten questions on a page, with just enough space between them (1 to 3 inches) to handwrite a postcard-size response. The spatial limitation was inviting. It made it a fun game. I'm a postcard writer and tend to fill all available space once I get going. The postcard gets written (letters often don't) and sent. Having limits is good!

No sooner had I finished the first group of ten questions than the next group arrived, again with inviting empty spaces, this time the questions ranging further afield from Contact into my personal experiences dancing, philosophies, views—on CI, performance, solo work, magazine making, love, life. I went along, amused to try to find and fit a response into the welcoming space. The exchange between us was of course as much about David as it was about me and my responses. After the third round of Q & As, we were in another place. Were we "there" yet? Did we have what we wanted?

By late 1994, we had two live interviews and three rounds of written Q & As. Good stuff, DK said. Too much for an article now; how about a book? And how about a few photos? Of you dancing? Maybe a few of you as a child? Your family? And what about a few of those "dance-in-translation" hieroglyphs you make? (We could use them for page numbers! I piped up, getting into it.) It was the classic Stone Soup story. From a single stone and lots of enthusiasm and curiosity, the ingredients for a hearty meal began to simmer.

David was excited to do this book, full steam ahead. I was already "four paws in" when I suddenly felt extremely uncomfortable and reticent to be co-creating a book with so much about me in it. But David was convincing. A devoted practitioner of Contact Improvisation, David wanted the message of "the work" to get further out into the world. He thought I was already a messenger with wings on my heels and miles behind and ahead of me—an ideal vehicle to get the ideas circulating in the world. No small matter was the tumor growing on DK's right optic nerve, benign but nonetheless threatening, already twice necessitating open-head surgery—a daunting ordeal to say the least. With his mortality put thus in the forefront of his attention came a strong desire to accomplish certain projects. Our book was one of them. I was flattered, intrigued, wary, excited, and curious to see how it might develop.

Meanwhile, who was my collaborator? Who was this David Koteen? At the annual Breitenbush CI Jam in Oregon, he was a full-bore physical, fanciful, smart, insightful, productive, creative, soulful fellow Contact Improvisation dancer, with whom I'd shared a good physical and mental sweat or two or three—both on the dance floor and in mineral hot spring conversations about dancing, life, art, language, heart. At the jam, he presented wonderfully odd, idiosyncratic performances with text and movement and props (wigs, mirrors, stepladders, scythes). I remember watching him and thinking, Wow, way out on his very own limb; bravo.

So it was David I went to for feedback when *Raku*—my tender ferocious super-slow heart-broken-open dance—was being considered for inclusion in a jam performance and I wondered, Is this really performable? This was only my second time considering performing this "movement state," and I didn't know how best to frame it into visibility without overriding its intractably slow development. Could I make this intimate dance a bit more presentable? David's deep seeing of its highest intent, along with his playfully serious and useful suggestions, helped move it—and me—along. Outside of these experiences, I knew little of David Koteen—until several Breitenbush Jams later when he approached me about *The Sun* interview.

As our discussions turned more seriously toward making all this material into a book, I wrestled with my doubts about making such a personal book and sought counsel. I added friends' and colleagues' voices to the book and worked with David on how we might balance all the elements that we had accumulated. Meanwhile, I continued to be intrigued with the process and what it was revealing about the work, life, and us. Ultimately my curiosity and pleasure in the collaboration won out.

photo: Mark Stone

Nancy and David establishing contact, 2000.

And so it was that my original agreement to talk about Contact Improvisation for *The Sun* had been played and parlayed by my perfect trickster DK, in the spirit of service and research, with my willing, amused suspension-of-disbelief into the making of this book.

Although *Caught Falling* is not a book about the dance form Contact Improvisation per se, it is very much an expression of that work, in the same way that most anything I say or do at this point is inevitably informed by three-plus decades of seemingly inexhaustible interest in and devotion to the practice and investigation of Contact Improvisation. While many of the questions and answers in this book address CI either directly or indirectly, it is in the free play of ideas, curiosity, questions, stories, humor, and imagination between David Koteen and myself that Contact Improvisation is most present in this book.

It has now been more than fourteen years since David approached me about *The Sun* interview. Children are grown, another optic nerve tumor surgery has come and gone, loves have been lost and found, many more dances have been danced. New material has been added and removed from the book and then added again. I am grateful to David for the opportunity this book has given me to put on paper and into language some of my thoughts, stories, and feelings about dancing and living. I appreciate his unwavering encouragement, time after time, to wrestle with and expose myself in the hopes that doing so will not only inform you of my life and practice but quicken and encourage your own.

Caught Falling is a book for you to enter anywhere, follow along with, skip around in, imagine your own answers to the questions, be amused, be informed, and enjoy in your own time. Follow the faces and the passage of time through a life; a family; and an extended family of relatives, colleagues, and friends. Imagine your life in it.

I have benefited beyond calculation from the profound teachings and enlivening practice of Contact Improvisation. Thank you Contact, thank you Steve, thank you David, and thank you contacters all over the world. May the benefit of our work and our pleasure in the dancing continue to multiply.

Nancy Stark Smith
2008

what is contact improvisation?

Because Caught Falling *is a book written more* from *the experience of Contact Improvisation than* about *it, we thought it only fair to offer readers who are not familiar with the dance form a clue as to what Contact Improvisation is. I have attempted to do this in as succinct and matter-of-fact a way as possible, lest this book take another fourteen years to finish! A more detailed history of Contact Improvisation (as told from my perspective) appears in* Contact Quarterly, *Volume 31#2, Summer/Fall 2006, as well as in stories and references throughout this book. Other resources for information about CI are listed at the end of this chapter. [NSS]*

WHAT IS CONTACT IMPROVISATION?

Contact Improvisation (CI) is, at its root, a duet dance form based on the dialogue of weight, balance, reflex, and impulse between two moving bodies that are in physical contact. The form was first presented during a series of performances that took place in New York City in June 1972 at the John Weber Gallery, conceived and directed by American choreographer Steve Paxton. Steve had danced in numerous modern dance companies in New York in the 1960s, including that of the revolutionary choreographer Merce Cunningham and his longtime collaborator John Cage, a major innovator in music and artistic thinking. Steve was also a prime mover in the groundbreaking performance work of the Judson Dance Theater in the mid-1960s in New York City, which was instrumental in redefining dance and opening up new possibilities for the art form—the where, how, and what dance could be. Steve's radical choreographic propositions in the sixties and his exploration of improvisation—solo and with the dance theater collective the Grand Union—all preceded his proposing of Contact Improvisation in 1972. For more on Steve's brilliant mind and work, you can read on and between the lines of this book, explore several decades of his writings in *Contact Quarterly,* and consult a growing number of books that address his enigmatic and important work.

I first met Steve Paxton as a young dancer at Oberlin College, in Oberlin, Ohio, when he came there as a guest artist in January 1972. Six months later, I participated in the first performances of Contact Improvisation in New York with Steve and others. Quite by surprise, Contact quickly became the focus of my life and work and has remained at the heart of my dancing life.

photo: Stephen Petegorsky

Steve Paxton and Nancy Stark Smith performing Contact Improvisation with Freelance at A.P.E., Thorne's Marketplace, Northampton, MA, 1980. (Daniel Lepkoff and Christina Svane in the background.)

From its early days on the East and then the West coasts of the United States, Contact Improvisation has spread to studios, schools, and art centers around the world. Many thousands of people have experienced this "shared moment of movement" and passed it on through teaching, through direct physical transmission, or just by example. Thousands have performed and demonstrated Contact and applied it to choreography; to dance training; to their work with children, seniors, disabled populations, therapy, visual art, music, education, environmental work, social activism, and on and on. Meanwhile, hundreds of new exercises, scores, theories, words, principles, formats, and performances have been created. There is no official certification for teaching CI; pedagogies have been constructed and reconstructed many times over in many studios around the globe. CI's influence can be seen throughout modern and postmodern dance choreography and performance worldwide.

Though its applications are constantly expanding, Contact Improvisation continues to be most vitally exchanged and developed in the dancing itself—in classes and jams, partner-to-partner, body-to-body.

DEFINITIONS

There is no single definition of Contact Improvisation. Defining the form in words has always been a challenging yet compelling activity. From the start, Contact's basic premise, its DNA, has been communicated most directly through the dancing. Words come after.

Though the physical and conceptual basis for Contact Improvisation, as given by Steve Paxton, was *experientially* clear from the outset, the language to represent it was not fixed. Rather, it too was played, improvised, and invented between dancers alongside the developing dance form.

In the absence of a single, official written definition of CI, contacters wrote their own, and authorship of specific definitions quickly became difficult to trace. Starting from the early years, we wrote and rewrote many different definitions for class flyers and performance posters—always feeling free to adopt, adapt, and invent new ways of describing the dancing phenomenon we were experiencing. In fact, throughout the first decade of *Contact Quarterly* magazine—a dance and improvisation journal that began in 1975 as a newsletter for Contact Improvisation—we published a different definition of Contact in every issue, along with a photo. This was done not only as a way to document and encourage attempts to put language to the evolving movement form but also as a way to discourage attachment to any one way of defining it.

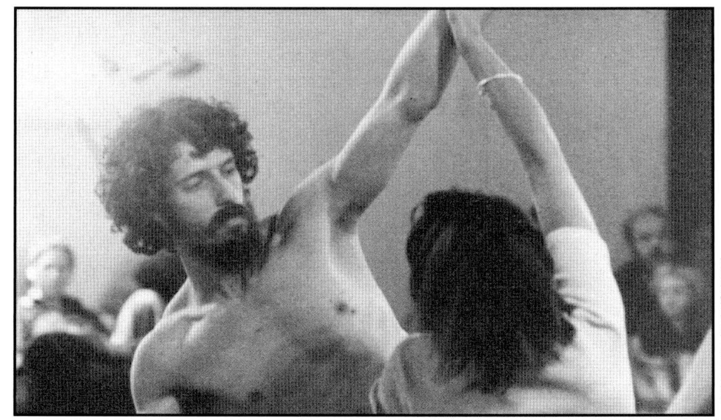

photographer unknown

Steve Paxton and Barbara Dilley dancing in the first performances of Contact Improvisation at the John Weber Gallery, NYC, June 1972.

Early on, one useful way of describing the new dance form was by likening it to better-known duet movement forms:

> *CONTACT IMPROVISATION is an activity related to familiar duet forms such as the embrace, wrestling, surfing, martial arts, and the jitterbug, encompassing a wide range of movement from stillness to highly athletic...*

Soon, definitions attempted to describe not only the outer form of the activity but also its inner focus. For instance, this lovely, simple one attributed to Curt Siddall in 1975:

CONTACT IMPROVISATION is a movement form, improvisational by nature, involving two bodies in contact. Impulses, weight, and momentum are communicated through a point of physical contact that continually rolls across and around the bodies of the dancers... Like bolos [sic], fluid and eccentrically weighted, the dancing bodies swing, bounce, roll, and fly through and with a common center.

One particular definition that I personally keep coming back to is:

CONTACT IMPROVISATION is a duet movement form, originated in 1972 by choreographer Steve Paxton, based on the communication between two moving bodies that are in physical contact and their combined relationship to the physical laws governing their motion—gravity, momentum, friction, inertia, centrifugal force, etc.

photo: Raisa Kyllikki Karjalainen

Nancy and Juha Viitamäki, Helsinki, Finland, 2007.

The simplicity of this notion—a dancing dialogue using touch, movement, weight, and balance to play the body and the physical forces with a partner—is both simple and expansive. Using this focus as the basis for my improvisation helps me stay clear about what I'm doing even as the experience inside the dancing grows more complex, stimulating many levels of thought and feeling. Including the physical forces as an integral part of the danced conversation gives me a clear structure and orientation to come back to over and over. Of course, we are not just "moving masses"; we are human beings. However, it is within the dialogue of moving masses grappling with the physical forces that human beings meet each other most vividly. Inside the dancing, we confront and adapt to differences in interpretation, timing, temperament, and technique. In other words, we improvise—not only "sharing the dance" but also creating it together.

I've always loved Steve's apt and pithy ways of pointing to the subtle interiors of the work. For instance, early on he wrote:

The exigencies of the form dictate a mode of movement which is relaxed, constantly aware and prepared, and onflowing. As a basic focus, the dancers remain in physical touch, mutually supportive and innovative, meditating upon the physical laws relating to their masses: gravity, momentum, inertia, and friction. They do not strive to achieve results, but rather, to meet the constantly changing physical reality with appropriate placement and energy.

And then there was dancer Simone Forti's delightful early assessment of Contact as an "art sport," a phrase that temporarily circumvented the "but is it dance?" issue. Her spontaneous moniker offered a fresh perspective on the young form, and it was used regularly for several years and still has currency today.

Perhaps it is not surprising that a movement form based on touch and the sharing of weight, balance, and impulse might run into trouble when it comes to recognizing boundaries—for instance, in the authorship of definitions, teaching methods, performance structures, language, and formats in the developing practice of the work. As Steve wrote in a recent email to me discussing how the form evolved:

I see it the other way around perhaps. The form was developing us... And earlier, there is a big issue of co-development. It is barely clear to my memory who brought what to the table. I knew this would happen; so many of us participating, so many years, so many classes and performances shared. I did my part, but in any group endeavor even a small suggestion may grow to large importance. I mean, I'm still grateful to Doug Winter for an Aikido roll suggestion [in 1972], for heaven's sake. Finally, there is just too much to be grateful for to be all that specific.

And in further email discussion about acknowledging individual strands within the fabric of the work, he replied:

We look around and see firm fabric but have no choice but to project our own strand, since we are all midstrand, as it were, and continuing the weave... I imagine all the strands are important, else no fabric.

Finally, a last favorite definition, an amalgam of several different early writings and voices (mostly Steve's) that touches on many important aspects of the work, both in concept and in practice:

CONTACT IMPROVISATION *is an evolving system of movement based on the communication between two moving bodies that are in physical contact and their combined relationship to the physical laws that govern their motion—gravity, momentum, inertia.*

The body, in order to open to these sensations, must learn to release excess muscular tension and abandon a certain quality of willfulness to experience the natural flow of movement. Practice includes rolling, falling, being upside down, supporting and giving weight to a partner. Alertness is developed in order to work in an energetic state of physical disorientation, trusting in one's basic survival instincts. It is a free play with balance, self-correcting the wrong moves and reinforcing the right ones, bringing forth a physical/emotional truth about a shared moment of movement that leaves the participants informed, centered, and enlivened.

photo: Bruce Newhouse

David Koteen and son Japhet jamming, Eugene, OR, mid-1990s.

photo: Ted Pushinsky

Nancy Stark Smith and Steve Paxton, with Collin Walcott playing tabla, at the *CQ* Benefit at Berkeley Moving Arts in Berkeley, CA, 1978.

As Contact Improvisation continues to grow—numerically and geographically—and diversify in style and application, the more important it is to have a clear concept, an orientation for the mind, in pursuing this dance form. Will Contact be able to maintain clarity, coherence, integrity, and depth as it continues to proliferate and evolve in the world? It is precisely because of the enormous profusion of vocabularies and approaches now present in the work that I often feel the need to return, through the many layers of accumulated ideas, to the simplest definitions.

When I asked Steve recently what he thought the "core proposition" of Contact Improvisation was, at first he said he didn't know, but on further reflection he offered this: *Do under others as you would have them do under you.*

Contact Improvisation is a gift that seems miraculously to keep giving. I give Steve enormous credit not only for bringing the form into being but for his openness, curiosity, and generosity in allowing CI's practitioners to participate as deeply as they wished in its development without copyrighting it or restricting its use. This has empowered the work and its participants immeasurably. We all have a lot to be grateful for, and I don't see this ending anytime soon.

Nancy Stark Smith

For more about Contact Improvisation—books, magazines, videos, and links to other CI resources—visit the Contact Collaborations website at www.contactcollaborations.com.

This conversation evolved from a series of exchanges—interviews in person or on the telephone, typewritten questions with handwritten answers, and longer letters. It is nonlinear and can be dipped into at any point where it catches your interest. [DK, NSS]

(Photo/Image credits are on pg. 108)

David: Hi, Nancy. Do you know who this is, calling from green and lush western Oregon?

Nancy: The voice of sanity.

✦

David: You knew I was going to call one day; well, today is perfect for the interview. Any strictly off-the-record comment you want to start with?

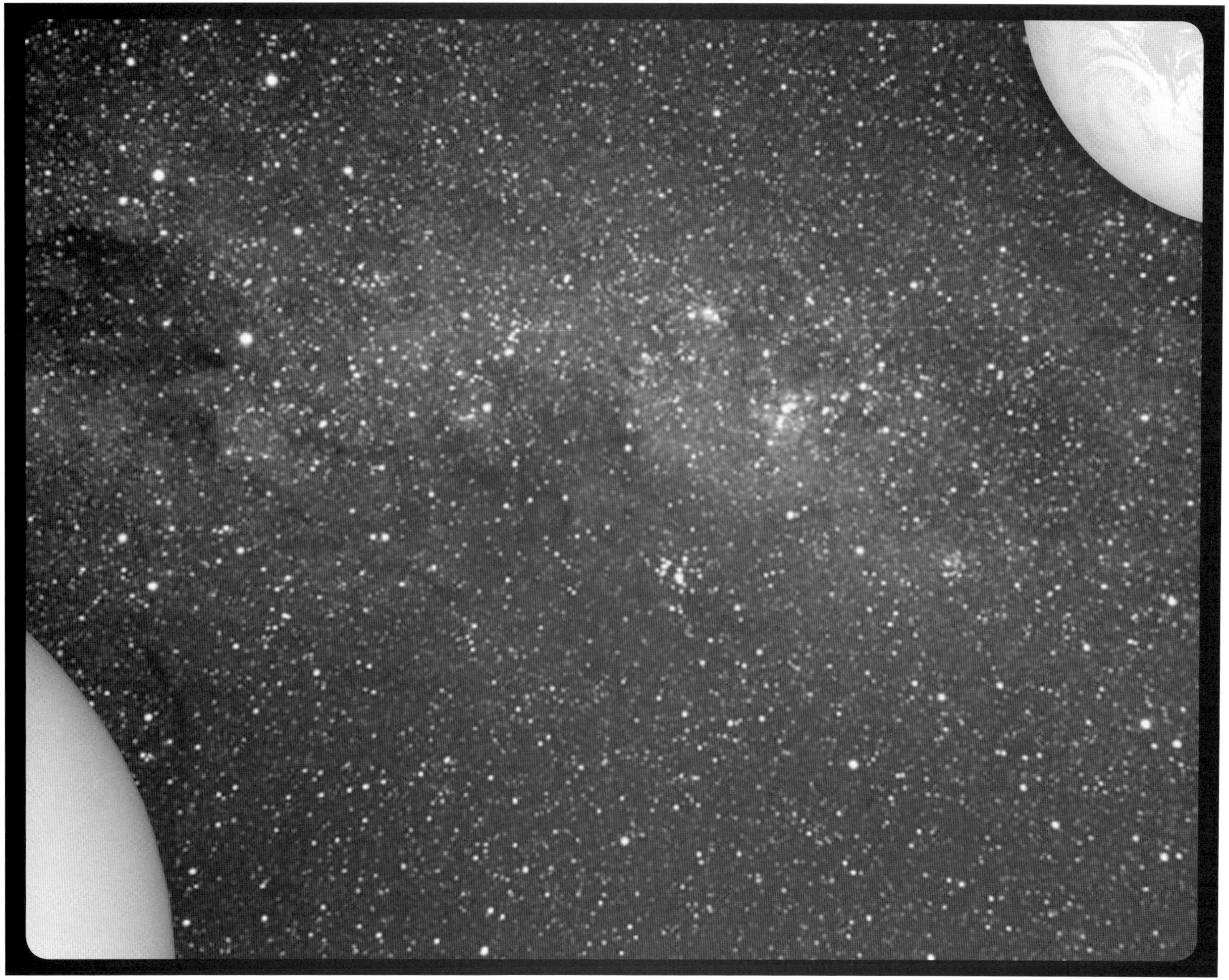

Nancy: The sky is blue with a variety of gray-tinged white clouds of different shapes and textures cruising out from the western mountain ridge, crossing the available Vermont sky at a medium clip. When the sun is out and I'm in it, I want to strip down to bare minimums; the next moment when it slips behind said clouds, I am pulling down raised sleeves, putting on second shirt, third, both long-sleeved. It is the transition from summer to fall in northern Vermont. Red-leafed branches are beginning to spot the wooded landscape but haven't yet taken over.

✦

David: Your long braid, "famous as a hero's horse" (C. Svane), is like a monkey's or squirrel's tail: an aid in flying?

Nancy: Yes, it can really swing, and it is a handy demonstrator of momentum, centrifugal force, "slack" and "taking out the slack," and other physical principles. It's also sometimes an unwitting partner or weapon. Otherwise, it

NANCY, 1978, ON NYC ROOFTOP IN THE EARLY YEARS OF HER "PERIPATETIC LIFESTYLE."

ROAD GOING UP. PHOTO BY BILL ARNOLD.

is my plumb to the center of the earth; a pal; something soft to hold, twittle, twirl, toss; a warm wrap around my neck; a pillow on a hard wood floor; easier to deal with than short hair. My disguise.

✦

David: In the early years of Contact Improvisation, language had to be developed to describe what it was that you were doing. How has descriptive publicity evolved?

Nancy: Early on, we either demonstrated physically or suggested familiar partner movement forms from which to imagine Contact Improvisation (CI)—"a cross between jitterbugging, wrestling, and making love." For a long time, and even still, definitions focused on the physical forces, like: "Contact Improvisation is a duet movement form based on the communication between two moving bodies that are in physical contact and their combined relationship to the physical laws governing their motion—gravity, momentum, inertia, centrifugal force, etc." Now, publicity is as varied in focus and style as the practitioners—terse and technical, otherworldly, psychologically soothing or tantalizing, poetic, innovative and arty, daring, dancerly, West Coast, East Coast, speaking to the recreational or professional movers. Hopefully there's enough linkage between all to imply a coherent work.

1952 Joe and Lucy's baby

The story goes that my mother, Lucy (Lucille Deborah Stark, then Smith), was already in fast labor with me when she and my father, Dr. Joseph J. Smith (Joe, or JJ), an obstetrician and gynecologist, drove to pick up Dr. Moe Glass, my father's mentor and a friend of the family, who was going to deliver me. They kept the car running as my father ran into the house to get him; Florie, Moe's wife, invited them in for something to drink. No time for that, my father insisted, I was coming NOW, let's go! No time to shave her (the custom at that time), they wheeled Lucy down the hallway at the Long Island College Hospital in Brooklyn, NY, with her clothes on, directly to the delivery room. I slipped out (second child) somewhere along the way, February 11, 1952. ✦

DAD AND NSS (17), 1969.

David: I often describe Contact Improvisation as an American martial art but with no defense. Comments?

Nancy: And no offense? Defense and offense are both communications that probably occur in CI too. But in CI, the intention of the activity isn't to fight or prevail over the other or to neutralize their aggression, but to dance together. Perhaps in CI you could call it action and reaction. Yes, like martial arts: always being in the ready state. Maybe it's closest to tai chi "push hands" practice, where you're testing each other's readiness to respond.

✦

David: One comment often heard from onlookers is that CI looks dangerous. What about fear and the body?

1957 Lucy's death

Lucy was a writer, had written plays in college at Brown/Pembroke, and was working for *Life* magazine when she met my father (the doctor). She was a researcher for the "*Life* Goes to a..." column, and she'd go with the photographers to the site—a debutante ball, spelunking, ice fishing—and write up the notes. During the late 1940s when she worked there, many wonderful photographers were at *Life*, including Alfred Eisenstadt and Cornell Capa. They seemed to enjoy taking pictures of Lucy, as I have a big folder of large lucid black-and-white prints of her in many of these adventures, with the photographers' stamp on the back. These have become precious contacts for me with the woman my mother was.

She died of breast cancer when I was five; she was thirty-five. ✦

NSS, LESS THAN A YEAR OLD, 1952.

LUCILLE DEBORAH STARK, NANCY'S MOTHER, ON ASSIGNMENT AS A RESEARCHER FOR *LIFE* MAGAZINE, 1946.

Nancy: It's relative. I don't want to hurt myself or others—physically or psychologically. Fear is a signal or, rather, an interpretation of a signal. If I can "hear" the earliest signal of limits approaching (physical, energetic, emotional) with enough time and confidence to address it and guide myself out of danger, then I can transform fear into heightened sensitivity and appropriate action. Onlookers' fears are often projected—they would feel at risk if moving like this. But contacters train to dance within their limits. So it's not as dangerous as it might look to watchers untrained in the dance form.

✦

David: Currently for me, intimacy is the new road, the work, the way. Intimacy and touch go hand and hand. And contrariwise, non-intimacy and non-touch lead to abuse and bayonets. As Karen Nelson has so aptly stated: Contact is the "touch revolution." Comment?

Nancy: In Contact Improvisation, you need to be able to harmonize with your partner physically and energetically to dance with abandon safely. To read and be read through the surface of the skin takes patience and speed. It requires being aware of yourself and the other at the same time, often sharing a common center of balance—synchronizing weight, rhythm, and

1950s Early home life and Ernestine Mary Baker Gomez Harris

After my mother died, my older sister, Susan (Susie then, or Oogie Mitt to herself when she was first learning to talk), my father, and I lived together for another five years before he remarried. As an obstetrician, he was regularly called out in the middle of the night to deliver babies, so we had a housekeeper, Ernestine, who lived with us. I loved Ernie and spent a lot of time with her. We colored together. Her style was a very light rubbing of the crayon color, neatly filling the whole shape to the line and never going over the line. Mine was more saturated color, more pressure, less precision. She gave me baths and had an intercom to my room (one floor below hers) in case I needed her in the night. Her skin was light brown and very, very soft, her teeth big and white, her lipstick shiny and deep red. I thought she was very beautiful.

When my father remarried, he and his new wife merged households over the summer when we were at camp (she had two children too: a boy between my age and my sister's, and a girl, older than my sister). When I returned from camp that summer, the merged family had been moved into a much larger home. Ernie wasn't there. The only explanation I got when I asked for her was that she had hurt her leg and might be coming later. I never saw her again, though I found her number in the phone book and called her. I continued to call her every year on her birthday (March 11) until she died when I was in college. ✦

NANCY WITH OLDER SISTER, SUSIE, AT HOME IN GREAT NECK, NY, c. 1959.

timing enough to proceed. This does tend to reinforce cooperation rather than aggression. In Contact, initiative can replace aggression.

✦

David: Again the question is raised: How does one get to a new place from the place where one presently is? Individually, from abuse to intimacy; culturally, from defense/victory orientation to compassion?

Nancy: Two images of getting to a new place come to mind: Herbert Guenther, Buddhist scholar/translator, once said (in a high voice with a heavy German accent): "Problems are never solved, problems dis-solve." There's also this feeling I often have that as I approach a problem, like approaching a wall, it gets larger, worse. "Oh, this must be the wrong path, it's getting worse." Then I realize that to get to the other side, I often have to pass through, up against, over/under the thing in question before it's really "behind" me. In any case, I

Camp and early movement memories

I started going to sleepaway camp in the Berkshire Mountains of western Massachusetts when I was six years old. I was in my element at camp—finding great pleasure being in nature; swimming in lakes; learning how to water ski, sail, play tennis, make fires, make silver rings (I still wear one that I made as a teenager there), be in plays, write songs, live with others. I was the editor of the *Log* one year, the campfire newspaper. A welcome contrast to suburban Long Island, NY. ✦

JOSEPH JAY SMITH, NANCY'S FATHER, CAMP DOCTOR AT CAMP GREYLOCK IN BECKET, MA, EARLY 1940s.

LUCILLE DEBORAH STARK, NANCY'S MOTHER, EARLY 1940s.

have to start from where I am before I can go somewhere else.

✦

David: "Love" is a word/idea that slips quickly into drivel; so entwined with Venus-Jesus-Penis-Parent-God-Knights and Maidens—I avoid it. But "gravity" is one that grabs me. Gravity approaches some terrestrial law, in a simple psychophysical way.

Nancy: Grabs you indeed, gravity. Try to stop it. Or rather, don't try to stop it! It is: profound, basic, assumed, not well used (when ignored), abused (when fought against), a beautiful sight to behold when integrated within the dancer's body's actions—like a string on a well-tuned instrument.

✦

David: Citing Lao-Tse: "Gravity is the root of all grace." Agree?

Nancy: Perhaps grace can be said to be the coordination of the body with the forces of nature (gravity, etc.). In CI, physical efficiency, all parts working in balance, makes grace. I think there's also another element of grace that has more to do with mind and attitude than physical forces.

THE FATHER AND MOTHER OF NANCY'S FATHER'S FATHER, NATHAN SMITH (GIVEN THIS LAST NAME ON ELLIS ISLAND c. 1900). THEY LIVED IN EASTERN EUROPE, SOMEWHERE IN WHAT WAS THEN EASTERN POLAND.

New York grandparents

My sister and I went into "the city" (NYC) regularly to visit our grandparents, Poppy and Elvy (my mother's father and second wife), who we were very close with. They lived on the East Side, on 63rd Street, with a good view of the East River from their apartment. I'd wake up early and sit at the table with a piece of paper, marking the passage of the boats—a big line for big ones, a short line for small. Elvy would take us to museums and other cultural activities. We called E66 Street "Egg" Street. ✦

NANCY'S HOME, 22 CLARK STREET, FLORENCE, MASSACHUSETTS, 1996.

David: One function of CI is to minimize cultural influence between dancers. I'm thinking: no music, no special clothing, no gender roles, no preset movement steps...

Nancy: It sounds pretty basic—and is. But when you put any two people together and ask them to touch and relax and listen to the information they're getting from the sensations in the touch—about how gravity is acting on the body, the play of physical forces in the movement—and to move in dialogue with all of this, a lot is being stimulated. Touching, as an activity, is tremendously culturally loaded. CI does offer a relatively neutral vehicle for exploring the exchange of movement and impulses through the touch—not particularly clinical, not necessarily social, but human and physical—but even so, we're never completely free of our cultural assumptions and patterns.

Best friends

My best friend until my father remarried and we moved to the other side of town was Cheryl. She was a year older than me and several times bigger, and I adored her. We'd play for hours and hours until we were fried and just had to take a break. "Good-bye and good riddance!" we'd exclaim proudly, having picked the phrase up somewhere. One day we were at Cheryl's house, diagonally across the street from mine, and after hours of being together, we'd had it. "Good-bye and good riddance!" I announced, and went storming out of the house with Cheryl slamming the door behind me. But the screen door was locked, and I distinctly remember holding the screen door handle, which was at the level of my mouth and nose, while the big front door slammed behind me. There I was, standing between the locked screen door and the front door unable to move. "Cheryl!" I called, "I can't get out!" Shocked, she opened up in gales of laughter. The "screen door story" became a family classic. ✦

JULIA GULACK SMITH, NANCY'S FATHER'S MOTHER, BORN IN RIGA, LATVIA, CAME TO THE U.S. AT AGE 13.

NANCY AT HOME ON THE SUNPORCH, GREAT NECK, NY, c. 1961.

AUGUSTA STARK, NANCY'S MOTHER'S MOTHER, PROBABLY ON SCHROON LAKE IN THE ADIRONDACK MOUNTAINS IN NY, SOMETIME IN THE 1930s.

✦

David: The cultural thrust of gender is immense, including almost all dance forms, following traditional male-female cultural roles. Contact?

Nancy: There is a lot that gets paired in the Contact duet. Gender is one of those things, sexuality another. Big and small get paired, experienced-in-CI and non-experienced, traditionally trained dancers and not, performer/not performer, younger/older, friends/strangers—many different differences get paired. In Contact Improvisation, one is invited to meet partners on many different fronts; gender is not necessarily the most important factor. More important might be how they respond to touch; the quality of their weight shifts; the timing of their impulses and responses; their risk factor; how they respond to quick changes, to falling, to supporting weight; their strength; the tone of their mass; their sense of humor, rhythm...

Certainly one's gender and sense of oneself as a man or a woman is present, but it is not necessarily the primary factor. It totally depends on the two people—their combined intentions and what the moment stimulates.

I'm her elder sister. I knew her first, *nyeh, nyeh.* You might say that was the story of our childhood. End of story? No.

Nancy, I'm going to "out" you. We grew up in Great Neck, New York. I can't give you an idea of the humiliation that statement carried with it but to say that in Great Neck there didn't seem to be any room for creative thinking or unique style.

Susie and Nancy. It was always somewhat embarrassing that my parents (surname: Smith) chose prenoms which were in the top of the baby boom hit parade. Stark was my mother's family name. Stark Smith suits Nancy better than Smith. Don't you agree? A reaction to the mundane.

So it's hard to know Nancy without seeing the *reaction* in her action. Here are some more facts: Our parents are both dead. Our mother predeceased father by 38 years. Nancy was 5. She loved the housekeeper who dressed her and brushed her hair each day. Then our Dad remarried. We moved. The dog was left out in the winter and died. We lived. Two, then three new siblings. We continued to survive. End of story.

Not all of Nancy is a reaction. In those turbulent years we absorbed a lot of positive attributes. My father instilled ethical values and standards for accuracy, honesty, righteousness, conscious living, and awareness of one's impact on others. Nothing was relative, everything absolute. My mother's legacy fades in haze. She didn't teach by example, but by rumor. What we heard about her. She was a writer of comedies for student productions at Brown University, became a wife and briefly a mother. Her last job was writing fun things for *Life* magazine.

All those themes converge in Nancy's work.

Nancy is clearly more than the sum of her parts. But the parts that converge make sense. Her natural ability to move, to think, to write, have been honed by experience. Her reactivity is central. Ready to judge each moment and act accordingly. Improvising to take advantage of each micro change in a situation. To mitigate falls and damage. Using strength, courage, and the ability to make instantaneous decisions that adapt to the world as it presents itself. And then talk about the experience. Everything fits.

Susan Smith Berenzweig
sister, psychologist
Mamaroneck, NY

SISTERS SUSIE AND NANCY ON THE FRONT STEPS AT HOME ON HEREFORD RD., GREAT NECK, NY, c. 1959.

NANCY AND NEPHEW ADAM BERENZWEIG (SUSAN'S SON), MAMARONECK, NY, 1978.

David: Talk about a Contact Improvisation jam.

Nancy: A meeting of minds on the dance floor, body first. A chance to improvise within the form of CI with a range of people at different levels of experience—an opportunity to speak this "common language" across regional borders and learn new moves and interpretations from the bodies of people you've never met. Or with known partners, to play through familiar or new territory. It's not a class. It's self-directed, a session for bringing what you've got and putting it on the line with others doing the same. An opportunity to improvise with the materials.

✦

Early memories of Lucy

My mother had, unbeknownst to me, been ill with breast cancer for quite awhile, probably since I was about two. She had had a mastectomy and wore bras with foam in them that I remember finding and playing with a few times. But otherwise, I just remember her being around the house, calm and lovely; in a lawn chair outside in the back, reading with some ice tea (in a tall frosted glass with red polka dots); or in bed. When I was trying to stop sucking my thumb, she'd sit on a chair next to my bed holding my hand as I fell asleep. I would try to outlast her so I could suck it again and was amazed by how long she sat there, in the silent dark, just holding my hand. I was SURE she must have thought I was sleeping, as I hadn't moved in a long time, but she just sat there and sat there for a long time holding my hand. ✦

NANCY AND NITA LITTLE PERFORMING IN SANTA CRUZ, CA, DURING REUNION TOUR, 1978.

David: Often people bring "agendas" to a jam, sexual or other. How do you deal with this? And when you say "putting it on the line," do you mean risk-taking with your body?

Nancy: Yes, my body is always the base, foundation, center point. As well as my ideas, interpretation. And yes—self-responsibility and awareness are key, whether it's about physical limits or emotional ones. If someone is approaching me with a kind of sexual intentionality that I'm not wanting or if someone gets very athletic or physically rambunctious and I'm just not in the mood, I need to communicate to him or her, preferably through my dancing, that I'm either not ready or not interested. Or, if it's possible for that person to continue what he or she is doing without implicating me too terribly, maybe it can work to have different styles and intentions. I don't necessarily need to stop the person, but I do need to communicate my situation and be able to dance within my limits.

✦

David: In Contact Improv, weight is constantly being transferred through the bones. CI is a dance of bones?

Losing Lucy

One day my father took my sister and me to the hospital and had us stand in a certain place on the grass and pointed to a balcony about four or five stories up and said to look there. He went into the hospital and emerged on the balcony with my mother. We all waved happily to each other for a while and then she went inside. Not long after that, we were in NYC with my grandparents Poppy and Elvy when my father called to bring us home right away. My sister (8) and I (5) were brought upstairs to my sister's room, and my father told us Mommy had died and that she wasn't sick anymore. He was holding back tears and then crying, my sister was crying, I was feeling a bit confused—on some level I felt relieved that she wasn't sick anymore, something was good about that, but I saw my father—my main loving guardian (and he was very much both those things)—unhappy and my sister too. I wasn't feeling what they were feeling and it scared me. I guess I didn't know that her dying meant I would never see her again. ✦

NANCY AND DAD AT THE PIANO ON HEREFORD RD., GREAT NECK, NY, 1958.

NANCY PRACTICING HER LESSONS, 1958.

Nancy: The skeleton gives form, structure; clean, easy support with minimal effort. Organs vitalize and juice up the play. Glands charge. Skin...so much information that it is sensitive to and transmits. Contact can engage all systems and has the potential for multidimensional, multiquality dancing and relationships. Bones are useful and clarifying to return to.

✦

David: I remember one time when you were dancing with your partner, and she kinda jumped, bumped over your back, and fell on the floor. You said something like, "What's so good over there that you're banging me and yourself to get to it?"

Nancy: I did? Hmm, I'm trying to remember the moment... I seem to remember feeling like we got out of synch and I felt her reaching for something outside the path of flow between us. Feeling the physical dissonance it created,

MATERNAL GRANDFATHER LOUIS STARK ("POPPY") AND SECOND WIFE, ELVIRA STARK, ON THEIR HONEYMOON, c. 1946.

BELOVED HOUSEKEEPER, ERNESTINE MARY BAKER GOMEZ HARRIS ("ERNIE"), HEREFORD ROAD, GREAT NECK, NY, c. 1959.

I wondered what it was, what was drawing her "out of the flow," against the grain. Sometimes it's a habitual movement pattern that diverts you out of the current flow of moments as they're forming and shunts you into a less custom-made option. Of course, the dissonant move could also be a conscious choice. But in this case it didn't feel like it was.

✦

David: What about dancing with heavy folks?

Nancy: One thing about doing Contact that seems liberating for people is that they are able to fully inhabit their mass and not shrink away from it because they feel that they should be other than they are. To feel their full weight and have an open and engaged relationship with gravity, to feel their weight directly in relation to other people, is freeing and gives both dancers the information they need to be able to make the necessary adjustments to handle it. Sometimes big people can feel extraordinarily light, and small ones very dense and heavy. It depends a lot on how you are handling your mass.

It's very empowering to develop skills that will enable you to responsibly process or handle a large person's weight, or even a small person hurtling at you or jumping on you—especially if you don't think you can support

NANCY AND SUSIE WITH GRANDPARENTS POPPY AND ELVY, HEREFORD RD., c. 1958.

I am Nancy's grandmother.

How can I tell you anything about Nancy without mentioning her mother, Lucy, who died when Nancy was five years old?

She had been on the staff of *Life* magazine on a special feature, "*Life* Goes to a Party."

She was very bright, gentle, loving, and caring and also full of whimsy.

All just words that do not at all evoke her aura.

She was very special.

How sad that Nancy was deprived of such a mother.

And how sad that Lucy can't know what a gifted, vibrant, warm, and loving woman Nancy has become.

It is I who enjoy her sporadic visits, her confidences, our little outings, our meshing.

She too is very special.

Elvira Stark
grandmother
Los Angeles, CA
(deceased Feb. 2004)

NANCY AND BEST FRIEND CHERYL GOLDMAN, GREAT NECK, NY, 1957.

them completely or for long. There are ways to sluff (slide) or redirect the person's moving mass that will communicate to them that you are "with" them but not able (or wanting) to support their full weight. It's not wise to assume you know what your partner's response should or will be to anything. The best one can hope for is honest, instantaneous, and direct communication. This is the nature of the dialogue.

✦

David: Here's a question: Contact Improvisation is the perfect metaphor for life?

Nancy: It's curious to me that people are surprised to see that their improvised dancing reflects their daily living. When you are doing Contact, you are behaving, basically, as yourself. In the dancing, you're manifesting/embodying your curiosities, your timing, your sensibilities. Different partners might draw out different aspects of your nature in the dance. Meanwhile,

NANCY WITH HALF-BROTHER DAVID CHARLES SMITH, AT HOME IN GREAT NECK, NY, 1970.

VARSITY CHEERLEADERS AT GREAT NECK NORTH SR. HIGH SCHOOL, GREAT NECK, NY, 1968. [1ST ROW, L–R] MYRA ROSENSTEIN, ILYA KALTMAN; [2ND ROW] LESLIE CLASTER, RONNIE TAFFET, AIMÉE GREENSTEIN; [TOP ROW] MARGIE BROWN, LYNN FEIGENBAUM, NANCY, MARCIE MURDOCK.

Late 1950s, early 1960s
A doctor's daughter

My father was ever-present in our lives, taking us for drives and special walks in the woods, where he'd leave little clues about where he was; making barbeques; always tracking our schoolwork; giving us "20 Questions" at the dinner table—"Who is the Secretary of State?" "What is a baby swan called?" He was an academic with extremely high standards. He was a teacher at the Albert Einstein College of Medicine and had always been a whiz kid. I was very proud to be his daughter.

Sometimes my sister and I would get to go to the medical school with him. He was always greeting everyone—from the doorman and elevator operator to interns and patients—surprising people with little hard candies in his handshake and introducing me proudly. One day when I was probably six or seven, he left me in a classroom with a big blackboard while he did his rounds. I spent the whole time standing on a chair, writing on the board; first, a line at the top explaining who I was and what I was doing there, and then... I don't remember what but I filled the board completely with words. In the room was also a worn-out model of a pregnant woman's pelvis, cut off at the waist and the top of the thigh, with huge rubber labia and a term baby in her belly. Delivery practice. The rubber was cracking and dusty when I snuck a try. ✦

it also becomes possible to notice your own habitual behaviors over time and decide to alter and experiment with them in the dancing (like intentionally responding in an unfamiliar way or initiating more if you tend to follow).

The nature and focus of the dancing duets vary tremendously from partner to partner and from dance to dance, passing through issues of physics, aesthetics, social/sexual matters, movement invention, thrill seeking, soothing, playing, research of many kinds, following the unknown, dance making. Situations that occur "in life" do show up in the dancing as well, and many aspects of the physical dancing (how close to your limits you play, the proportion of supporting/being supported in your dancing, how you relate to un/familiar movement vocabulary when it presents itself) can easily be seen as metaphors for your life. In fact, they *are* your life.

✦

NANCY AND STEVE PAXTON, WITH COLLIN WALCOTT PLAYING TABLA AND JEW'S HARP, PERFORMING AT THE *CQ* BENEFIT, BERKELEY MOVING ARTS, BERKELEY, CA, 1978.

Father and physicality

My father was always very affectionate and physical with us. Many of the home movies we have from our early childhood show him giving us piggyback rides, hugging us on the end of the diving board and then throwing us into the pool, showing off jumping over a hedge as we watched, putting us up on top of the refrigerator. One game I loved and asked for over and over was being flipped over on the bed. I'd lay on my back at the edge of the double bed and curl into a ball, and he'd put his hands under me and, at the count of three, throw me high into the air so I'd flip over and land on the other side of the bed on my belly or back (depending on how fast and how high he flipped me). He also used to swing me from his neck; I'd clasp my hands around his neck and he'd bend over and swing. He found it hard to refuse me, even when I had become too big for it; he ended up in a neck brace with several cervical dislocations. ✦

David: What do you mean by "physical states"? What's an example of how you work with them?

Nancy: A physical state is a particular experience of body/mind generated by engaging in a particular physical activity, usually for a sustained period of time.

For instance, in CI we work with a spherical sense of space, training the senses (seeing, hearing, moving, feeling gravity and touch) to be comfortable while the body is moving through different positions relative to the ground. One trains in falling and rolling and rising and turning and being upside down and spilling through the sphere slightly off-balance, in a continual flowing momentum, playing with and being played by gravity. Doing this activity for several minutes, or hours, generates a condition in the dancer that could be called a "state."

Or, another example might be doing the "small dance" of standing—standing still quietly, observing the body balancing itself on two legs,

"The Pretzel!!"
"The Suitcase!!"

We would like to share our early childhood early morning memories of our aunt Nancy.

Julie remembers the Pretzel, a Nancy-original game that was a (barely concealed) pretext for tickling. Forming human pretzels out of her niece and nephew involved all of the culinarily correct stages: kneading the dough; rolling the dough; and, of course, folding the pretzel. The memorable punch line: salting the pretzel, which was just flat-out tickling. Needless to say, after the salting, the pretzels had somehow lost their shape...

Adam remembers the suitcase packing game, in which Nancy's belongings (a few shirts, underwear, a toothbrush—all of which bore a strong resemblance to her niece and nephew) were bundled into a blanket. The squirming package was then slung over Nancy's shoulder and toted to her destination. Often, Nancy would take a pit stop to retrieve some vital item from the bundle: "Where's my toothbrush? *I know* I put it in here..." From inside the bundle, a shaft of light would stream down, carrying with it the tickling end of aunt Nancy's arm. The toothbrush was usually found to be hiding under Julie's ribs, only after a thorough search through Adam's armpits.

We guess that Contact has always drawn a fine line between dancing and playing. For us, it was just about playing, and we feel lucky to have been packed, kneaded, salted, and rolled by such a unique playmate.

Adam and Julie Berenzweig
nephew and niece
New York City; Boston

[LEFT TO RIGHT] STEPMOTHER CAROL SMITH, NEPHEW AND NIECE ADAM AND JULIE BERENZWEIG, NANCY, FATHER JJ SMITH, SISTER SUSAN BERENZWEIG, MAMARONECK, NY, 1987.

sensing the micromovements the body makes to keep its weight balanced over its supports... a kind of physical meditation practice. Doing this activity for 5, 10, 15, 20 minutes creates an overall quality of mind and body that could be called a state. It's not only about how your body feels doing that activity but what mood it induces in you.

There are of course innumerable states that could be identified: slow-motion, tantrum, loose and floppy (in body and/or mind!), slow and sensual, athletic, energetic, strong, light and ethereal, quick and reflexive, coarse, quirky, refined, playful, cautious, and erratic. Each different quality of physical activity generates different energetic and psychological states.

✦

David: How did this understanding of physical states affect your teaching?

Nancy: I realized after years of teaching Contact Improvisation that in the course of doing the dancing I found myself in many different energetic states—some deeply internal, meditative, grounded; some full of momentum and abandon; some slow and delicate, light and airy, fluid, bouncy, solid, and so on.

I also noticed in teaching that certain physical skills were easier (or harder) to do from one particular state or another. For instance,

Merged household

My father remarried when I was ten, entering us into a new phase of family life. There were some positive aspects—playing basketball with my stepbrother and his friends in the driveway; a new half brother, David—but for the most part, the merged household was a stressful one, the atmosphere tense. I stayed away as much as possible, opting for more compatible surroundings such as after-school sports, volleyball, gymnastics, cheerleading, poetry club, and madrigal choir. I would time it so that I'd ride my bike into the driveway just minutes before 6:00 dinnertime. ✦

NANCY AND DANIEL LEPKOFF PERFORMING WITH FREELANCE AT RIVERSIDE STUDIOS IN LONDON, ENGLAND, 1981.

after a long period of doing the "small dance" standing meditation—feeling one's weight deepen into the earth, feeling gravity's pull on the body's mass and sensing the support rising up from the ground through the substance of the bones—students would definitely not be ready (read: in the mood, physically inspired) to throw their mass lightly into the air toward a waiting catcher. So if we were going to practice throws and catches or lifts, it might work better if we transitioned into a state more conducive to tossing ourselves in the air.

The transition between the states became quite interesting for me. I'd find myself kind of conjuring a change in the appetite in the room through a combination of images and activities—perhaps a little shaking out, "fluffing up," un-sticking the particles of our mass, bringing some easy loft and "levity" (opposing force to gravity) into the body—and some lightness would begin to happen, as if the body substance had actually, physically and energetically, changed state. And from there we'd start the throwing and catching exercise.

NANCY AND ANDREW HARWOOD PERFORMING IN NORTHAMPTON, MA, 1984.

School years, athletics

Throughout my school years I was an insatiable athlete, loving the physical rigor and interplay of team sports. I also was attracted to gymnastics, especially the equipment, learning more and more cool moves (the uneven parallel bars were my specialty) and eventually beginning to compete. I much preferred learning and doing the movements to competing. I loved feeling the rush of the swinging arcs and circles, overcoming the fear of letting go of my hands as my body curled around the other bar, the amazing integrity of the physical forces and the feeling of riding them. In team sports, I was a fierce competitor, committed to winning but not at the expense of our team spirit. I have to admit that even though I dislike the tension of competitive play, I've never really stopped wanting to win when playing sports. ✦

COURTYARD TREE. PHOTO BY BILL ARNOLD.

✦

David: Is this what you mean by "changing states"?

Nancy: Yes. I began noticing that these changes of image and activity affected not only people's physical movement qualities but also their moods. Faces would brighten, people would get outwardly radiant or lighthearted during lightness-evoking activities or become more internally focused, concentrated, and serious when involved in deepening or grounding activities. So I began to study, empirically, these relationships—noticing the physical/emotional/energetic states that would arise, seeing what activities might catalyze what changes, and noticing if there were any patterns.

It was interesting to realize that it could work both ways—you might be drawn to move with a certain quality because you were in a particular mood, or by arbitrarily changing the movement quality you were doing, you could change your "mood" and thus your desire. So when improvising, you needn't feel at the mercy of moods for access to movement qualities or states; you can just generate the appetite for them yourself, maybe just by starting to do them!

This approach to "changing states" has often been helpful in assisting people in learning certain physical skills and having access to

DURING REHEARSAL AT THE OBERLIN DANCE COLLECTIVE IN SAN FRANCISCO, 1978.

First dance

In high school, I remember seeing the dance club practicing in the room across from the gym, all the girls lined up in black leotards, looking at themselves in the mirror as they did tiny bending movements of their knees. What, I wondered, could be the appeal of this? It seemed a narcissistic, physically minimal, and unsatisfying activity. Obviously, I didn't join that club.

I don't know how or why I got there, but I did end up going to some local dance classes in town as a teenager. As well as teaching us set, stylized movements, one day the teacher asked us to choose either a scarf or a ball and make up a dance with it. My first improvised dance! (I chose the ball.) ✦

certain qualities or states that they might not normally get to by themselves. Generally, though, I find that Contact Improvisation dancing takes care of a lot of this by itself. Just by following the dance you'll find yourself inhabiting many different states.

✦

David: What's a Contact high like?

Nancy: Every part of me feels very alive—turned on, awake, present, ready, both comfortable and on my edge, sharpened and softened, deepened and extended, challenged and soothed—physically and energetically tuned to myself and others. I'm directly in dialogue with my environment. Moved—body, mind, spirit, imagination, humor, heart—and in motion. Inspired.

✦

1960s Finding bohemia

In high school in the 1960s, I found myself in two worlds: the "straight" one, wearing the print-skirt-cardigan-sweater combos bought for me at the Berkshire Coat Factory when my parents visited at summer camp, in honors classes, on sports teams, and at temple, and also attracted to the "off" track lifestyles, people, and "bohemian" life I was introduced to at my friend Tana's house. Tana's parents were divorced (unusual among the people I knew), and her mother was an artist—a cartoonist—with a dry, acerbic humor and wit. The house had a large open floor plan with a big round oak table in the kitchen; newspaper clippings and cartoons stuck up on a bulletin board; the Sunday *New York Times* spread around the couches all week; a Chemex hourglass paper-filter coffee pot on the stove; jazz playing on the stereo; and cats all around. Her mother, always seemingly in a state of semi-despair, complained constantly about everything, but to me she was amusing and interesting. I always felt seen and related to as a person by her; and though life was a drag and a problem for her, she did it with an intelligence and a creative twist that I always enjoyed. The art on the walls, the music in the air, the hip cousins that came through, the informal but creative atmosphere, were very attractive to me—I felt stimulated and at ease. I liked many aspects of these two worlds, and each seemed to balance the other; I never felt a need to have to choose between them. ✦

NANCY WITH SUSAN SCHELL'S SON, EV, DURING REHEARSAL FOR THE POST-BREITENBUSH JAM PERFORMANCE AT WOW HALL, EUGENE, OR, 1989.

A CAPPELLA MOTION FACULTY PERFORMANCE BOW, A.P.E., THORNE'S MARKETPLACE, NORTHAMPTON, MA, 1994. *[LEFT TO RIGHT]* ALITO ALESSI, HILLEL KRAUSS, SUSAN SCHELL, KJ HOLMES, NANCY, KAREN NELSON, CHRISTINA SVANE, DANIEL LEPKOFF.

David: Describe the process of coming together with Steve Paxton et al. to investigate this young unformed entity: Contact Improvisation.

Nancy: Appetite. Pleasure. Stimulation. Investigation. Fun. Immersion. Engagement. The rush of a new bud opening.

It was a great group. A few of Steve's colleagues were there (Barbara Dilley, Mary Fulkerson, Nancy Topf) and some other young dancers like me whom he had met as a guest artist at Oberlin College, the University of Rochester, and Bennington College over the years. The work was fascinating, fresh, absorbing.

The first week, we had all-day "rehearsals" in a loft space. We trained on a small blue wrestling mat in the loft of a friend of Steve's for the first week, with occasional sessions in Battery Park and other grassy spots. Hour after hour of rolling technique—forward rolls, backward rolls, aikido (diagonal) rolls, handstand roll-downs, back walkovers, and other gymnastic moves that anyone might suggest, spotting each other for safety. Steve would lead us through long stints of "the small dance of balancing," a standing meditation that has remained an important part of CI. These "stands" would go on for fifteen to twenty minutes or more at a time, stretching the endurance of our concentration with meditations on balance,

Going to Oberlin

For several years in junior high, I had a French teacher whom I loved. She was a beautiful young woman, with long hair that she wore in a variety of styles—sometimes down, sometimes twisted up, or in combinations. I loved watching her elegant, capable hands work the tape recorder and slide projector in the middle of the room as we had our "audiovisual" lessons. She had gone to Oberlin College in Ohio, and I liked the way she talked about it. As expected of me, I applied to various "good schools" on the East Coast for college, including Pembroke (Brown University), where my mother and aunt had gone and where my sister was currently enrolled. Instead, I decided to go west to Oberlin, as far west as I had ever been, to a landscape flatter and wider than anything I had ever experienced in New York or New England, and to an environment that promised to meet me in unexpected ways. ✦

POST-BREITENBUSH JAM PERFORMANCE QUARTET AT WOW HALL, EUGENE, OREGON, LATE 1980s. *[LEFT TO RIGHT]* ALITO ALESSI, RICCARDO MORRISON, KAREN NELSON *[BELOW]*, NANCY.

the bones, and the scale of movement. This rigorous contemplative practice tuned us to the subtlety and intelligence of the reflexes of the body, which in turn became the foundation for the more overtly disorienting flinging and flying of bodies in space that we would practice on the mats.

The other training activities in that first week in NYC included throwing and catching practice. In these sessions, the catcher would stand toward the back of the blue mat with one foot slightly stepped back, to make the eventual spiraling motion easier to initiate. One after the other, the individuals in the group would run and jump into the air in front of the catcher, hoping to be caught. The catcher would snatch the falling mass against his or her body, sometimes turning to follow the momentum into movement, often going down to the mat with the mass and following through with a roll ("turning vertical momentum into horizontal travel," Steve later wrote). We practiced and watched jumping and catching for many hours each day. Sometimes we'd be led in head-to-head dances, in which

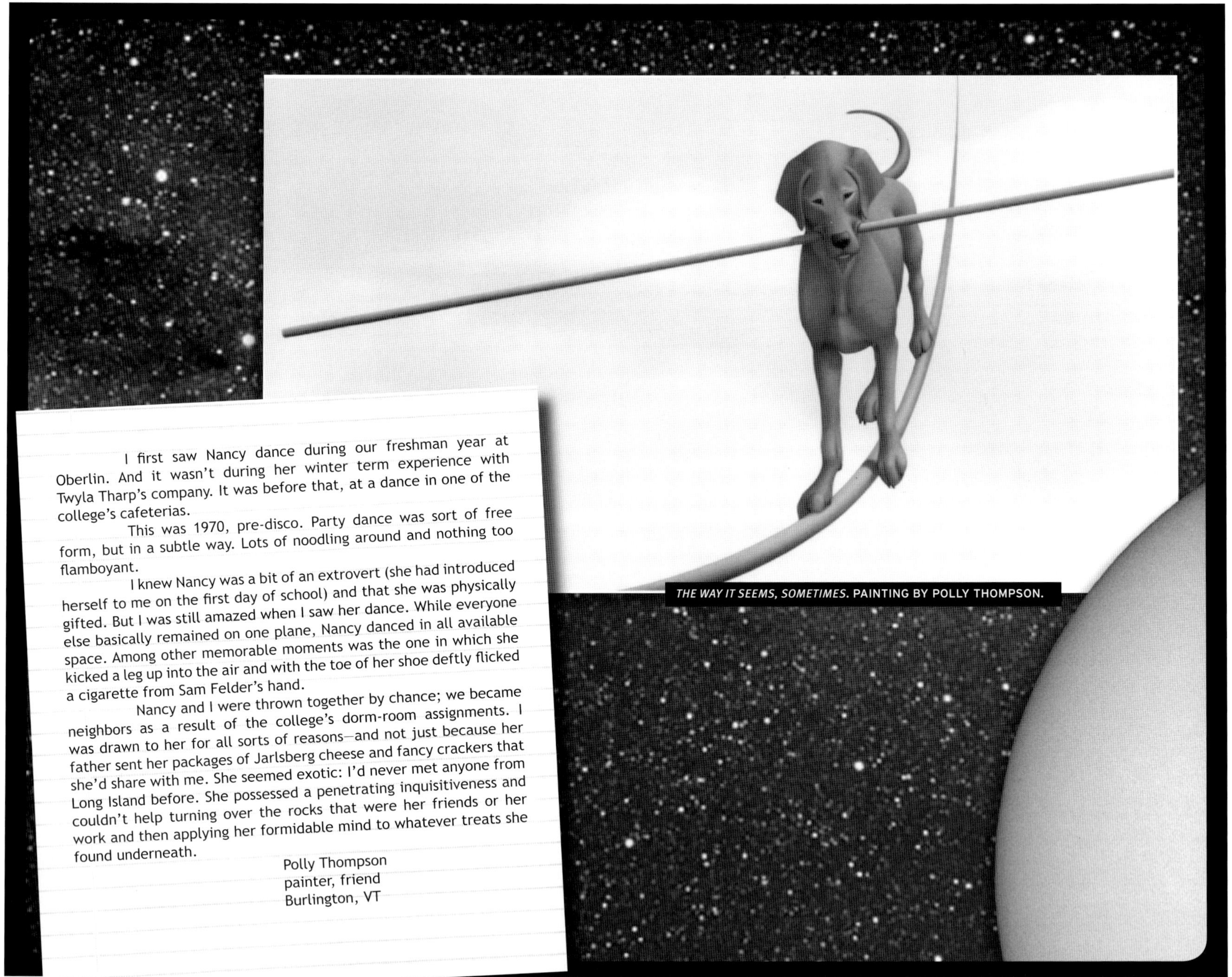

THE WAY IT SEEMS, SOMETIMES. PAINTING BY POLLY THOMPSON.

I first saw Nancy dance during our freshman year at Oberlin. And it wasn't during her winter term experience with Twyla Tharp's company. It was before that, at a dance in one of the college's cafeterias.

This was 1970, pre-disco. Party dance was sort of free form, but in a subtle way. Lots of noodling around and nothing too flamboyant.

I knew Nancy was a bit of an extrovert (she had introduced herself to me on the first day of school) and that she was physically gifted. But I was still amazed when I saw her dance. While everyone else basically remained on one plane, Nancy danced in all available space. Among other memorable moments was the one in which she kicked a leg up into the air and with the toe of her shoe deftly flicked a cigarette from Sam Felder's hand.

Nancy and I were thrown together by chance; we became neighbors as a result of the college's dorm-room assignments. I was drawn to her for all sorts of reasons—and not just because her father sent her packages of Jarlsberg cheese and fancy crackers that she'd share with me. She seemed exotic: I'd never met anyone from Long Island before. She possessed a penetrating inquisitiveness and couldn't help turning over the rocks that were her friends or her work and then applying her formidable mind to whatever treats she found underneath.

Polly Thompson
painter, friend
Burlington, VT

we balanced our weight/bodies head to head and, maintaining the balance, felt our combined "small dances" and let this lead us into an improvisation while remaining head to head. Then we'd take turns doing extended "contact improvisations" in duets on the mat. These dances, watched attentively by the others, were improvised interactions. They were contact improvisations exploring what was possible with two people in physical contact, moving with each other, throwing, catching, sliding, falling, rolling, balancing, exploring what was possible while moving in tandem with another body within the gravity system. We experimented with how to take and give support; move and be moved; play with the physical forces of gravity, momentum, centrifugal force, friction, and so on.

All these early sessions were recorded by videographer Steve Christiansen, and we studied the tapes at night. Our work took on a rhythm of noticing variations, trying them the next time, and discerning useful physical principles, such as:

- It's easier for your partner to catch you if your center of gravity is positioned higher on the catcher's body and if the arc of your jump peaks at the catcher's body
- Turning falls into rolls
- Finding a variety of strategies for staying in contact with your partner
- Using the arms and hands as extensions

Finding dancing

Oberlin has a Winter Term program during the month of January—a month where students choose a special project to participate in, either on or off-campus. On advice from a friend, I enrolled in a dance project with the choreographer Twyla Tharp and her company while my best friend Polly painted. The daily schedule of technique classes and rehearsals was rigorous beyond anything I had ever experienced physically and, from the first day, mind altering. Twyla was pregnant, in her third trimester, and it didn't stop her a bit. She was intense, demanding, witty but not warm, focused, fascinating, and nonstop. Aside from teaching a strenuous neo-ballet class, she had us doing all kinds of movement for her. I remember doing a phrase that I think I made up, with several dive rolls and slides executed exactly within the seven seconds she had allotted for it as one of several hundred phrases interwoven and timed to the second in the performance piece she made.

One day in class we were instructed to look at Rose (one of Twyla's main dancers), who was standing by the barre. I waited for her to begin her phrase of movement as she shifted her weight a little, scratched her nose, straightened her shirt, and looked over to the window. "OK," Twyla said, "repeat that." *Repeat what?* I thought. *That* was the dance phrase? I discovered with great excitement that dance could embrace many kinds of movement, and unlike the competitive sports that I was finding less and less poetic and engaging, the dance art world was outrageously interesting and curious to me. ✦

NSS SOLO PERFORMANCE AT NAROPA INSTITUTE, BOULDER, CO, MID-1980s.

BELOVED HOUSEKEEPER #2, IVY VICKERS, AT THE HENHAWK ROAD HOUSE IN GREAT NECK, NY, 1986.

of the back—as leads into the rolls or slides on bodies rather than as grabbers and manipulators

• Listening to the forces inside the movement—your own and your partner's—as well as reacting quickly

Through the give-and-take of the dual dancing, new permutations arose and uncharted territories of the dancing were exposed. Individual styles were already emerging, and the possibilities were beginning to be fleshed out. Miraculously, there were no serious injuries, just plenty of black-and-blue marks.

After intense, rigorous experimentation and training for a week, we brought the mat to the John Weber Gallery in SoHo in downtown NYC and held our practices there. For five hours a day (in two chunks) for five days, we did "Contact Improvisations." Periodically, Steve would lead us through a "small dance" meditation; sometimes we'd practice rolling or jumping and catching, but mostly we engaged in extended duet dancing. A duet might last anywhere from five minutes to forty minutes.

At Oberlin

Brenda Way, the young dynamo dance teacher at Oberlin, saw me in Twyla's residency and invited me to join the Oberlin Modern Dance Company. I began to choreograph my own pieces and to take daily company classes in modern dance technique (Graham, Humphrey, Hawkins). The Graham Square. Contractions. Triplets again! Ugh, those torso circles. Didn't like it! Couldn't wait to have the teacher look away so I could dance the rest of the way across the floor as I wanted. But Brenda was an inspiration to me. I loved her breathy, swoopy, "undercurve-shift"ing Hawkins-based technique; her fun Twyla-esque choreography at the time; and her maverick, can-do generative style. If Brenda hadn't plucked me out of Twyla's workshop to join the Oberlin company, I wouldn't be dancing now. ✦

STEVE AND NANCY AT THE KITCHEN TABLE IN STEVE'S HOME AT MAD BROOK FARM IN NORTHEAST VERMONT, 1989.

NANCY AND STEVE PAXTON AT THE STINSON BEACH, CA, COMMUNE WHERE NANCY LIVED; PALM SUNDAY, 1978, BEFORE LEAVING TO GO ON TOUR.

When it completed itself, two more people would go out on the mat. At some point during the week, our appetite for dancing and our comfort with the activity had increased sufficiently that we simply pulled the mat out of the way so that more duets could dance at once on the bare floor.

People would pass through the gallery over the course of the day, some pausing for a few minutes to watch the moving bodies before continuing on their way through the gallery, some sitting down on the floor and observing the dancing for minutes or hours, some returning several times during the week. George Manupelli's *Dr. Chicago* movies, in which Steve was among the cast of characters, were also being shown at John Weber that week (during our breaks).

Over the next years, we continued to notice more aspects of the phenomenon of Contact Improvisation as we continued to practice it. Pickup engagements and tours happened over the years with Steve and others, forming a continuity of developing work and our relationship to it and each other, and teaching and performing and articulating ideas over the years. It was a really good time—big, yet easygoing. I received a lot of empowerment from Steve. From day one he encouraged me to be myself at my most natural, creative, smart, and independent. He expected it—and demanded it.

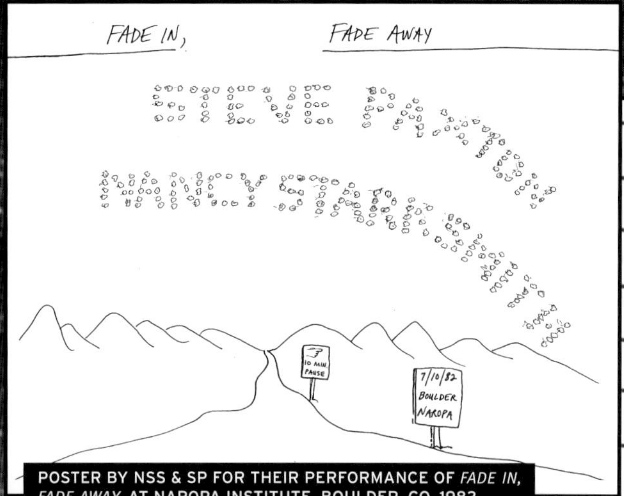

POSTER BY NSS & SP FOR THEIR PERFORMANCE OF *FADE IN, FADE AWAY*, AT NAROPA INSTITUTE, BOULDER, CO, 1982.

Writing and dancing at Oberlin—a choice?

After years of floating through a fantastic liberal arts education of classes in genetics, art history, religion, dance, literature, and eurythmics, I finally declared a dance and writing major in my last year of college.

My wonderful writing advisor, Stuart Freibert—always excited to the point of jumping out of his chair by some innocent turn of phrase or image I had managed to get on paper—was extremely encouraging of my emerging voice.

But when both my dance advisor Brenda and my writing advisor Stuart independently advised me to give up the other thing if I really wanted to be successful in my field, I was stumped. It was like having to choose between eating and breathing; I needed both to survive. Luckily I didn't have to choose but instead graduated. ✦

STEVE AND NANCY PERFORMING AT AND/OR GALLERY IN SEATTLE, WA, 1975.

David: Can you recall the taproot of Contact Improvisation?

Nancy: The taproot was Steve and the influences and interests he brought to bear on his work—such as the rigor, intelligence, invention, social politics, artistic philosophies, and high artistic standards of John Cage, Merce Cunningham, and Robert Rauschenberg, as well as Yvonne Rainer and his other Judson Church cohorts. He brought his background in modern dance, tumbling, martial arts, yoga, meditation, dance making, performance, improvisation, and living on a farm in a remote area of Vermont. And also Steve's own particular brilliance—witty, unpredictable, pithy, terse, imaginative, smart, dry. Always with a twist, an innovation, a new way to approach something. Did I say funny?

✦

David: If Steve is the taproot, what part of the CI plant are you?

Winter of 1984—I'd moved to NYC a year and half before. No more dancing—I was going to write music-theater. Still, Nancy asked me to assist her at Naropa Institute, making a piece with students and directing it together.

Nancy my Levitating Ponytail! Instructor in Empty-Full! She needs me! Because she's an improviser and she DOESN'T KNOW how to make pieces. I'll help her.

It was a good time. Snowy boots and coffeehouse conferences. Speedy, awkward skiing. Buddhists. I skipped Contact classes, staying at home to write a series of imaginary letters for the piece: a long-ago settler is wagon-training west in the Gold Rush; he gets to the Rockies, then waits forty years in Boulder for his beloved "Dear Cousin" back east, writing her faithfully though she never shows up.

Rehearsals were quizzical but fun. No one seemed to mind the pioneer romance, the simple-harmony folk songs Nancy and I taught the group, or the classic cowboy songs we used as underscoring. No one minded because they were dancing with Nancy. As the terrain of the piece came gradually into view, she introduced the movement-forms she'd been imagining: *Wheatfields*, *Crystals of Longing*, *Searchlight*, *Room Tilting*, *Starbursts*, *Waterwheel*, *Tipping Loop*, *Moo*. When we rehearsed these, I could not believe how precise were their effects.

We searched together for the piece. Threw the *I Ching*. One rehearsal, we asked each performer to list "things you are, and things you are not." "I'm not very sexy," Nancy wrote, and "I'd rather be too hot than too cold." I wrote, "I'm not the kind of person other people think is a jerk."

She drew a mountain range on the back wall of the Boulder performing space in masking tape as the set and wanted to call the piece "Cardboard Caravan." I wanted "Nameless Warmth," the pioneer's dog. We settled on *Cardboard Caravan, Nameless Warmth*. I was pleased with the compromise, though I still felt there was too big a gap between the phrases.

To fill out the program, we danced a duet. Music from *The Will Powers Institute: Adventures in Success*. Light pop-rock parodies about building self-esteem, complete with deadpan instructional role-plays. Odd, sweet. A big relief after the drama of westward expansion.

Andy Warshaw
composer, friend
New York City

ANDY WARSHAW *[ABOVE]* AND NANCY PERFORMING AT THE A CAPPELLA MOTION WORKSHOP, SMITH COLLEGE CREW HOUSE, NORTHAMPTON, MA, 1984.

Nancy: I would be one of the first green shoots (and green I was!). "The pleasure of moving in a spontaneous way," Steve says about the point of Contact, in the *Fall After Newton* video. Well, that surely was true for me. I adored the activity and the whole investigation. I watered the new plant with my attention, intelligence, enthusiasm, and body. I helped it grow and influenced certain directions in its development. Communication and articulation within the work—through dancing, teaching, performing, writing/publishing, talking, listening—have always been of great interest to me, and many of my initiatives led in those directions.

✦

David: In early Contact times, what kind of feedback did you get? Media coverage? Dance scene responses? Friends? Family? Other?

Nancy: Flushed faces, excited minds and bodies. Awe. Boredom. Questioning: Is this dance? Curiosity and eagerness to try it.

Media coverage? There was some, as Steve was already a figure in the dance scene and this, Contact Improvisation, was his latest investigation. There were a fair number of previews and articles about the existence of CI in local newspapers and magazines where we'd go. Mangrove—an all-men's Contact and theater

NANCY AND CURT SIDDALL PERFORMING WITH REUNION AT THE SAN FRANCISCO MUSEUM OF MODERN ART, 1976.

improv group from San Francisco—provoked a flurry of media in the early 1980s.

The "dance scene"? The avant-garde always responded positively. Certain individuals within traditional dance circles appreciated the work, but otherwise there was relatively slow acceptance within the traditional and academic dance scenes. Now, Contact is largely accepted as a technique for dance training, often to be applied to set choreography. Interest in improvised performance and the notion of dance as a "practice" is increasing but is still not tremendously embraced in more traditional dance circles. Certainly in meditation communities, the idea of a "practice" is well understood and appreciated.

✦

David: Sometimes dancers speak about "the practice" of Contact as distinct, shall we say, from the performance of Contact.

CURT SIDDALL *[LEFT]* AND DANIEL LEPKOFF PERFORMING WITH REUNION AT THE *CQ* BENEFIT, BERKELEY MOVING ARTS, BERKELEY, CA, 1978.

January 1972, a month away from 20; Steve Paxton, a soft class, a small dance

I met Steve Paxton in January 1972 when Brenda Way, with her brilliant, cutting-edge eye, invited the Grand Union to come from New York to Oberlin to work with us for the month. The Grand Union was an extraordinary, avant-garde dance/theater improvisation group with an all-star cast—Yvonne Rainer, Steve Paxton, David Gordon, Barbara Dilley, Trisha Brown, Douglas Dunn, Lincoln Scott, and Nancy Lewis—a company of individuals who had been pushing the boundaries of dance since their Judson Church Dance Theater work in NYC in the mid-1960s.

I think I must have been in all of their classes, swimming in a new world of art concerns, approaches, and behaviors—loving where I was without a clue where that might be. Steve's Soft Class at Oberlin that Winter Term began in the cold, early morning darkness, in a big old wooden gymnasium that was being used for the Grand Union dance residency, and ended when the sun came up. It was a very small class, and the three or four of us who made it through the cold, dark northern Ohio winter morning to the gym would find a chair by the door with a box of kleenex and a dish of cut-up pear or other fruit. We'd take one of each, entering the dark gym. During the hour of class, Steve would lead us in quiet standing meditation, focusing on the sensations of balancing, breathing, sensing the "small dance" of our standing bodies. I'd slip in and out of consciousness in the activity, in the dark, with Steve's low hypnotic voice guiding our attention to our body's sensation, the light in the room beginning to arrive, until by the end of the hour, the sun was streaming through the windows and class would be over. I was touched by this experience in a way that sometimes made me want to weep though I didn't know why. ✦

Nancy: They are in each other. It's a question of emphasis.

✦

David: I've heard people say, "Contact Improvisation is fun to do, boring to watch."

Nancy: So is: baseball? football? What makes something interesting to watch? For whom? Experienced contacters may see a lot of interesting detail and microchoices or macrocontextual choices or physical invention, outcomes of phenomena—both subtle and gross—in watching others dance CI. Or seasoned watchers and practitioners may be easily bored, having "seen it all before," not enjoying the repetitions or subtle innovations. Meanwhile, newcomers may thrill at basic phenomenon and miss details/subtle distinctions entirely. Or they may be bored, thinking/feeling that it all looks the same, whereas an experienced dancer may see significant and interesting differences in style and approach. I think a lot of Contact's viability as performance rests with the presence/power of the performer. Likewise, it depends on the availability of the watcher to be engaged.

✦

June 1972

20 years old and a major turning point

A few months after his residency at Oberlin, Steve invited me to be part of a two-week performance project in New York. So in June 1972, I arrived in New York City for Steve Paxton's project—"Contact Improvisations," the postcard announcement for the John Weber Gallery show called it. The postcard had an image of the Parachute Jump at Coney Island on it, and Steve also had a bunch of fortune cookies made in Chinatown with an announcement for our show at the gallery as the fortune. In our week of rehearsal I remember long periods standing still doing the "small dance"; rolling practice on a blue wrestling mat (forward, backward, diagonal, aikido, handstand roll-downs, etc.); throwing ourselves at each other and catching everyone; and many hours improvising continuous duet conversations based on touch, weight, balance, and so on. The second week, we performed for five hours a day for a week at the John Weber Gallery in SoHo, downtown Manhattan, mostly single duets at a time, watched by the rest of us. Gallery goers would come and go, some just passing through, some staying for several hours, some coming back repeatedly. These were the first performances called Contact Improvisation, June 1–5, 1972.

I remember this time as being a flood of newness and powerful direct experience. We were together all day long—doing and watching hours of dancing, then watching it on video, talking informally about the work constantly. We lived communally in a NYC Chinatown loft for those first two weeks, and the energy of the work followed us into the streets, our dreams, our showers, our food prep. It was total immersion. ✦

PERFORMANCE AT NAROPA INSTITUTE, BOULDER, CO, 1984. *[LEFT TO RIGHT]* TOM TRENDA *[ABOVE]*, KAREN NELSON, NANCY, STEVE PAXTON.

David: Could you talk about the origins of the *Contact Newsletter* and its subsequent growth into *Contact Quarterly*?

Nancy: It happened at a meeting in Stinson Beach, California, in 1975 with the early CI dance company ReUnion—Nita Little, Curt Siddall, Steve Paxton, and me—and my fellow communard Koriel, who was eager to help us get organized. At this time we considered copyrighting the name "Contact Improvisation" because we had heard of people getting injured from trying it without any training after having seen a performance. In the end we decided not to copyright it, as we were sure it would squash the work's radiant growth and meanwhile make us eternal Contact Cops.

At Koriel's suggestion (and another communard's access to a xerox machine), we started a little newsletter among us: What's up with the dancing, who we were working with and where, how it was going. Koriel and I took

A few NSS snapshots:

A hot Washington, D.C., summer day, 1975. Nancy and I go to National Airport to pick up her friend who is coming to teach with her at American University this Contact thing they do. I'm going to take class with them and find out what it is. We're in the busy terminal, and suddenly she hides behind a pillar. Then she runs out and jumps onto Steve Paxton, who catches her—they're laughing. The joyful swirl expands.

It's spring 1977. We're driving north above San Francisco, on the way to where Nancy teaches a weekly Contact class, and she's thinking out loud about what she'll be doing in the class that day. We arrive in a bedraggled little town (Point Reyes Station). I'm wondering who from here would come to Nancy's class? But I am not a Californian, and about six people ooze in from the muddy streets. The class is just like a big-city class—relevant and present and unbounded in scope. Satisfying. Then we head on to my friend's mountaintop scene. The steep nine-mile dirt road is a mess: it's been raining. Her jeep almost gets stuck. She is fearless and unflappable. I realize my friend has a strength and positivity beyond what I'm used to. I'm almost scared.

A culinary gift from NSS: a summer visit to her apartment; she brings out a bowl of cut-up watermelon and squeezes fresh lime juice on it. Since then, I never eat it without the lime and without a gentle flash of her in my heart.

A first-aid gift from NSS: she's visiting me and we're at our local pool. My son Jesse is a toddler and gets stung by a yellow jacket. She procures a cigarette, spits on the tobacco, and puts it on the welt—all better!

Ellen Cohen
BodySynergy codirector, friend
Ardmore, PA

NSS SOLO AT NAROPA INSTITUTE, BOULDER, CO, MID-1980s.

it on. His interests took him elsewhere after the first issue; I continued. I used the typesetting equipment (IBM Composer) of Diane di Prima, a poet and small-press publisher to whom I was apprenticed at the time in Point Reyes Station. A small "Contact Fund"—consisting of 5 to 10 percent of Contact teachers' net earnings (at that time about eight or nine teachers altogether)—paid for mail-out and supplies (and, later, xeroxing charges). After the first year (five issues) the fund was gone (few ever contributed), and we started subscriptions.

Letters led to short essays and drawings. More people than just the contributors started wanting copies. The Contact work was growing, and more people began participating in the newsletter as writers as well as readers. From the very beginning, we shared info in the magazine about other kinds of like-minded movement work in addition to CI. Three hundred copies (a few years into it) warranted offset printing instead of xeroxing.

I took the magazine production and business office wherever I traveled to dance, in my jeep and then in my pickup truck. I made issues with various collaborators in different places. Lisa Nelson stabilized as coeditor and coproducer by the end of the 1970s, with production sites in our homes. Eventually we started renting a room for six weeks, three times a year, for issue production—we'd come in like gypsies with card tables, makeshift light tables,

End of summer 1972, Massachusetts, continuing Contact

Though we all finished those first two weeks in New York quite flushed and excited by the "Contact Improvisations," few plans were made for continuing. But two of the factors responsible for the spreading of Contact Improvisation were already present: the desire to continue and the need to create partners to do it with.

At the end of that first summer, several of us ended up in Amherst, Massachusetts, with Steve, dancing daily on the grassy public commons and at night drawing pictures of the newly exposed movement pathways on the bodies (such as the figure eight and a half around the shoulder girdle, behind and in front of the head and the two arms); giving and receiving extensive massages; and dancing naked, greased from recent massages, in Curt Siddall's backyard on the soft layer of pine needles there. Rather a hysterical sight, we tried over and over to gain purchase on our partner's slick body but would inevitably slip off and emerge covered with pine needles—another informative experiment. ✦

QUARTET IN *DANCING IN MOVING PICTURES. [LEFT TO RIGHT]* NANCY, ANDREW HARWOOD, KAREN NELSON *[ON TOP]*, ALITO ALESSI, AT NAROPA INSTITUTE, BOULDER, CO, 1986.

and a typesetting machine; do the issue; and then move it all out, putting the setup back in the closets and under the beds until next issue. The office was in my home until 1985 when we got our first year-round office—in Northampton, Massachusetts, where the base is still located.

✦

David: If you were to fantasize—in your dream of dreams—the effect of CI on Western culture, what will you project?

Nancy: More peace. Flexibility (improvisation) based on a direct sense of being on the physical earth, in your physical body; communicating with respect, intelligence, curiosity, compassion, humor, and love across boundaries (race, language, ideology, dance form, cultures, subcultures, generations). Clarity, confidence, risk, respect. And more: cooperation, imagination, vitality. High art play, adventure in work, responsibility, and humor. A sense of independence and interdependence.

January 1973

Revolving around and within improvisation

I was smitten with Contact Improvisation, with Steve's approach, and with the other downtown artists in NYC. From then on, through 1973 and my junior and senior years of college, most of my school breaks were spent with Steve and whatever small group he'd gathered to present his new Contact Improvisation work. In January 1973, a year after meeting the Grand Union artists at Oberlin, Steve, Curt Siddall, Nita Little, Karen Radler, and I did our first tour of Contact Improvisation on the West Coast, around the San Francisco area and L.A. The name of the tour was, "You Come, We'll Show You What We Do." ✦

NITA LITTLE AND NANCY PERFORMING IN THE FIRST REUNION TOUR, NATURAL DANCE STUDIO, OAKLAND, CA, 1975.

✦

David: Is CI healing something(s) in our/U.S./Western culture?

Nancy: Touch and movement can be powerfully good medicine anywhere, I think. Especially when they come with a willingness to listen to what lives/moves under the touch and to meet that life with a benevolent, creative, albeit not intentionally therapeutic intent. Dancing—embodying impulse and perception, curiosity, creativity—liberates. At the moment, it doesn't look like Contact is having a very visible effect on our Western culture or politics as a whole, but maybe it's on its way up to the surface.

✦

David: CI as white people's self-expression?

Nancy: It's largely white, yes, though there are ever-increasing numbers among Latin and Asian populations. But I wonder if the contexts in which it is presented and the slant of the practice as it's offered might be partly responsible for this. When presented as a dance form (and not a social community function) in different countries (Asia, for example), it is taken to with real gusto, albeit with a little initial surprise, amusement, shyness. But so far

1974 Naropa

I had heard Baba Ram Dass speak in college and was excited by his message and his manner, enough so that I followed him out to Naropa Institute in Boulder, Colorado, right after I graduated in 1974. There I encountered Naropa's founder, Tibetan Buddhist teacher Chögyam Trungpa Rinpoche, and was introduced to meditation and a range of other Buddhist and Hindu teachings that would become an important part of my life. Also at Naropa, I picked up the threads of my writing training with Allen Ginsberg, William Burroughs, Diane di Prima, and the other Beat poets who were in residence. I found Diane's disarmingly candid and vernacular style penetrating and attractive. During one of the many poet parties held that summer, I overheard Diane saying that what she most needed now was someone to transcribe her journals. A fast typist, already four-paws in this swirling world of art and spirituality, I offered my services. She invited me to come back to northern California with her and apprentice her while transcribing her journals. With my Toyota LandCruiser full of all my college belongings, I continued west to California, where I lived for several years. ✦

NANCY STICKING HER HEAD OUT OF THE SUNROOF WHILE DRIVING TO COLORADO, 1984.

there have been notably few African Americans or black/Africans who have been attracted to Contact Improvisation.

The intimacy of the form (touching) may make it initially unattractive across community boundaries. This has been overcome with awareness and some initiative across several different subcultures—between sexual preference groups, between disabled and nondisabled movers, and between professional vs. non-professional dancers. It's of course dependent on people's actual desire to extend one's dancing experience across these borders. It takes initiative, desire, and circumstance. Also, CI isn't and needn't be for everyone.

✦

David: Let's say your weakness is your strength. In you, what would that be?

Nancy: A sad and tender heart. Other strengths often mask this vulnerability. Another strength that for me can be a weakness is the ability to

NANCY AND LISA NELSON MAKING AN ISSUE OF *CONTACT QUARTERLY* IN NORTHAMPTON, MA, 1984.

appreciate many sides of the same issue (and often, not so easily discern my own).

✦

David: I've heard *Raku*, your evolving solo, described as "fluid sculpture...both mercurial and clayey...both sculpture and mass." Do those comments seem consistent with your intention?

Nancy: They describe the outer manifestation produced by an inner focus that has nothing to do with any of those designations. Inner focus: core heat, heartbreak, lava flow; life force, flow through joints and tissues; slow, instructing which way to twist, turn, release, open, stretch, till "perfect" organization of body wants no further change—stillness, inner circulation throughout the shape. Until, again, the force moves and suggests change. A strong yet delicate flow. Tragic, painful, joyous, free.

Raku is an evolving physical form, or state. It evolves slowly. Now I can even stand up and maintain it! I used to only be able to do it lying down or sitting. But if I move at a more "normal" speed, I can't track this force. I felt the heat of *Raku* first in my heart and pelvis; the connection between those two centers animates my core and radiates out to make the *Raku* form.

Angels in West Marin

My time in California was spent living on the coast at Stinson Beach, just north of San Francisco, in a commune of gay men who all had angel names from their previous association with a spiritual commune—Koriel and Kiliel and Ehmroiel. At the request of my curious communards, I offered my first public classes in Contact Improvisation at the Dance Palace in Point Reyes Station, near where Diane lived. The first few years of the *Contact Newsletter* (now *Contact Quarterly*) were created in Diane di Prima's office on her typesetting equipment in Point Reyes. Among other things I learned from Diane was how to typeset books, strip corrections, layout pages, use an IBM Selectric composer, and justify type.

Thank you, Diane. ✦

FREELANCE PERFORMING *RAFT*, AT A.P.E., THORNE'S MARKETPLACE, NORTHAMPTON, MA, 1980. *[LEFT TO RIGHT]* CHRISTINA SVANE, STEVE PAXTON, NSS, LISA NELSON, DANIEL LEPKOFF.

David: Very joyful, Contact, is it ever?

Nancy: Ever! Often! Funny, very ticklish, very delightful. And one feels the absence of that just as often. We suffer in dancing as we suffer in life. Like, Where is it? How to tune, what do you do? And if it doesn't seem to be happening in a good way, how to deal? What choices? Withdraw presence? Initiate change? Working with principles from the aikido mind, which is deeply woven into this work—to merge, blending with the "other," and then, from inside the merge, to be able to redirect or suggest another direction.

✦

David: Like the dervish's spinning—a meditation?

Nancy: Yes, meditation in action, in the sense that one is watching the mind watching the body engaged in activity. In CI, the physical contact is the reference point. You can feel

KAREN NELSON, SANTA FE, NM, 1987.

Dear Nancy,

From the wonder-world of super shoptalk, where you and I have known ourselves to ponder such questions as "what is weight," I've been thinking about the conundrum of your "score." I wonder about calling it a score. If it is a score, it seems to be a jamming score, a way for people to focus and dance together with a beginning and an end. This is no small feat. After all, "the score" is usually done in non-jamming contexts, so trying to create a jam atmosphere in a class can be as difficult as trying to be funny.

I think of scores as activities—physical activities, like the score for Contact Improvisation, or the group score of closing the eyes and finding our ways into a circle. In these scores the participants are attempting to do an activity, and a dance occurs almost by default. The dances that these scores create will be completely varied depending on the particular dancers, yet the nature of each score will create similarities as well.

Related perhaps to the puzzle of naming "the score" [now called the Underscore] are my questions related to participating in it during two distinctly different periods of my dance life, which parallel different periods in its life and development.

The first period was when I was studying with you for the first six years of my Contact exposure. This was before "the score" was a score, and you led classes using all those elements that later became "the score." The scoreless score way of dancing in your class had a primary influence on my dancing soul. And I so love Contact jamming. To me, jamming is beauty. Is it because jamming is an intrinsically wonderful, natural kind of activity, or did I learn HOW to jam by cutting my teeth with your score, which at the time was not a score but a way that you taught Contact Improvisation?

In between this first period of working with the score before it was a score and the second period of revisiting the score as a score was a period of not studying with you. In my learning process I was yearning for definition, asking myself "What AM I doing?" What is Contact Improvisation??? Your classes became more vague, as you in your research were allowing the gap of knowing and not knowing to widen into vast chasms. As you were going forward with your questions, I had to go back to the roots of the work, to Steve Paxton's images and proposals. There I found what seemed to be essentially Contact Improvisation. I could distinguish IT from other forms of improvisational dance that I was concurrently immersed in discovering. Although I heartily agree that within a Contact dance all the choices of composition and games of perceptual improvisation and layers upon layers of body awareness and bodywork as well as all means and methods of communication possible through our bodies and minds are all there anyway, the clarification of forms helped my teaching and my various practices immensely. I started to look at Contact Improvisation as an underlying technique, as an intelligence that my mind and body could rely on. I continue to simply enjoy it as a practice to the utmost degree.

(continued)

when you've lost contact, lost touch. A wake-up call. This single focus helps keep your attention one-pointed, especially as an initial focus for training. Later, other points of awareness can be added to the mix, and partners don't need to be in physical contact all the time to maintain continuity.

✦

David: How do you divide/categorize "beginner" material from...?

Nancy: For me, there are two categories of contacters: people who have never practiced it before (in a jam or a class or anywhere) and those who have. Those who haven't need orientation to touch, gravity, flow, floor, senses, falling, sharing balance, ground, safety, rolling, moving through spherical space, inversion, joints' limits, sensation, efficient skeletal support, sliding, giving weight, supporting a partner's weight, dancing in a continuously changing balance with another, meeting, subtlety, the "small dance," following a point of physical contact, sensing and respecting limits, and *improvising* in contact—dancing, not just executing moves.

Beyond that, all of us who do Contact continue to learn and grow as we go along, attempting to remain safe and engaged within the expanding and refining exploration.

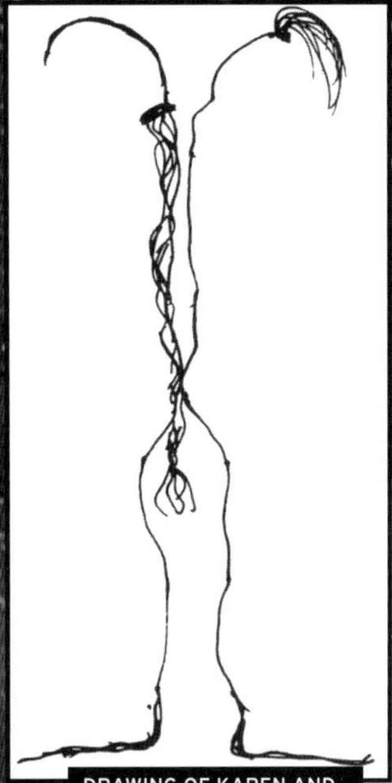

DRAWING OF KAREN AND NANCY BY SUSAN SCHELL.

KAREN *[JUMPING]* AND NANCY IN THEIR PERFORMANCE, *EVERYTHING MUST GO*, NORTHAMPTON, MA, 1989.

(continued)

For three years now we've been taking each other's classes in our Moving's View workshop. I meet "the score" (hey, don't I know you from somewhere?), with its incredibly detailed look at possible moments one passes through—from warming up to dancing with a partner to dancing with a room of people to a jam. There exists a precise language that you have developed to name many of the possible states that a human mind and body might encounter during a run.

My puzzle has been trying to work with it like I usually work with scores. I try to focus on the activity. But there are really no activities outlined in the score. There are names for states that could happen during this particular run and may not happen during the next particular run. On a rough day with the score, I find myself second-guessing my being. I wonder, for example, if I've "arrived energetically," or if I should abandon my interest in my partner-of-the-moment because I should be "grazing." You know, that kind of head stuff. On a sublime day with the score, what works for me is to simply do what feeds me, to really track my interest at the moment. I give that to myself as an activity. Even if that means, for example, to not walk with the group when you make the suggestion that we all start that way. If I'd joined, I'd have been a sack of disembodied, malnourished moving. I include myself in it mentally and stay embodied, present, and interested in my moving the whole time. At the conclusion I feel satisfied, healthy, and fed. Afterwards I can review or "harvest" what happened in terms of the score's language and its states. During practice, there are flickers of recognizing the score: "ah, this is an 'engagement'!" or "I think I just got 'grazed' on," as well as moments of simple total knowing of what the score means, the whole room of dancers being connected in awareness. This feeling of dancing is translated in my body as a complete ready-state, ready and open for anything or anybody on any level, be it physical, emotional, psychological, compositional, energetic.

The score seems to me more like a "changing states practice" and reminds me of the *I Ching: Book of Changes*. One does the improvisation and then interprets it afterwards through the lens of the how-ever-many-by-now states you have distilled and named. I think you should call it the Score of Changes in honor of its astute awareness and applicability to any of life's improvisations.

Love,

Karen Nelson
dancer, colleague, friend
Goldendale, WA

David: Training for CI in the beginning versus now?

Nancy: Current students of Contact are often surprised to learn that the earliest training sessions of CI with Steve included only about three or four kinds of preparations, such as the "small dance," rolling practice, stretches, throws and catches, and head to head dances, and otherwise lots of hours doing and watching the duet contact improvisations spontaneously danced by the participants. None of the now-familiar exercises of "tables," "posts," "bridges," "rolling point of contact," spirals, "surfing," "finger ouija," "sluffing/sliding," specific lifts, shoulder "orbits," or other movement patterns later isolated for teaching.

Without a set pedagogy to follow, Contact teachers adopt and adapt what they were taught, invent their own CI teaching methods, and also bring in materials from other disciplines (BMC, yoga, Laban, developmental movement, release technique, chi gung, modern dance) to serve the needs of the class. Much has

California commune

A baby was born in the commune. All the gay men were godfathers; I was a godmother. First thing every day, after tai chi practice, I'd put the baby (Arcenciel, or Ciel for short) on my back and walk down the beach to the post office, where the early *Contact Newsletter* had a P.O. box. Walking home on the road, I had a sense of space and light that I had never known on the East Coast: monarch butterflies clinging to the lush greenery, the wild nasturtium everywhere, "scratch and sniff" eucalyptus acorns, the smell of those wonderful little white alyssum that still remind me of California, and the glorious winding drive along the coast from San Francisco to Stinson Beach that I could do in my sleep (and sort of did some late nights driving home). ✦

NANCY AND CURT SIDDALL PERFORMING WITH REUNION AT THE SAN FRANCISCO MUSEUM OF MODERN ART, 1976.

been created, generously given, and eagerly absorbed in the growth of this movement form. And it continues.

✦

David: Staying in spiral is key to CI safety?

Nancy: *Follow-through* seems to ensure finding a way to play out the physical energy of the dancing (e.g., a fall) rather than having it hit a dead end (floor, joint), thus impacting unhappily into either body. Curvilinear forms work well for continuity and follow-through. The spiral is in that family. The beauty of the spiral is that it moves in several dimensions at once—for example, around and up and down. Other forms and rhythms can work too. But the subtle sensing—of gravity, balance, sensation, falling, muscle firings, joint limits—seems to be the major factor enabling the dancer to steer clear of trouble in enough time to avoid injury and keep dancing.

✦

David: People have to be in a certain state to receive the medicine, I say. What do you think?

Nancy: Two quotes from my early dreams come

NANCY WITH FREELANCE IN *RAFT* AT RIVERSIDE STUDIOS, LONDON, UK, 1981.
[LEFT TO RIGHT AROUND BLANKET] LISA NELSON, STEVE PAXTON, CHRISTINA SVANE, DANIEL LEPKOFF.

What's it like to be on a volleyball team with Nancy? She brings a dancer's grace and a linebacker's intensity to the game. She's competitive enough for the whole team. And she's fluid—she moves to the ball quickly and seamlessly, with a minimum of extraneous movement.

And when the ball comes back unexpectedly, and some of us (who shall remain unnamed) are standing around, flat-footed, watching it, Nancy mutters, while running for it at top speed and still managing to give the rest of us a dirty look, "Well, um, if no one else is going to get that, I guess I'll have to..." And she puts the ball up, and the game goes on, and we try not to start laughing until the point is over.

Randy Bartlett and Merry Nasser
longtime volleyball teammates
Northampton, MA

to mind: "Vibrate at disappearing frequencies," and "Perfect volume enters easily."

✦

David: One phrase/concept from your teaching that has always resonated strongly with me is "Replace ambition with curiosity." Could you explain this further?

Nancy: This is a phrase I've found myself saying fairly regularly over the years when teaching Contact classes, usually while people are dancing, as a way to encourage them to motivate their movement through their curiosity and desire to learn; to investigate, be surprised by, and discover their current dancing moment rather than making choices based on the pressure to achieve something or only to execute certain skills successfully.

"Replace ambition with curiosity" is an invitation to relax, to use the energy that might otherwise be taken up in worrying about getting it right, to follow one's curiosity and imagination in pursuing what it is that is actually arising. Discover

PARKING METER AND SAWHORSE. PHOTO BY BILL ARNOLD.

Summer 1975 Straw mats in Rome

We went to Rome to L'Attico Gallery, where Steve was invited by Fabio Sargentini, the gallery owner, to perform. After seeing the brick floor of the gallery, Steve organized a transformation of the space with straw mats from the marketplace layered with thin foam rubber lengths covered by more straw mats and eventually topped with a large sewn canvas sheet. A regular part of our Contact practice became straightening out the canvas surface after each dance had wrinkled it up. ✦

NANCY AND LISA NELSON, *CQ* EDITORS, ON THE COVER OF *THE VALLEY ADVOCATE*, A LOCAL NORTHAMPTON, MA, NEWSPAPER, JULY 1981.

it. Penetrate. Play. Dance. Invest in what's there.

Certainly the motivation to achieve, to learn, to try something, to master a skill, is positive and desirable. But it can often overwhelm the subtler curiosities and creative impulses and create stress. Opportunities that arise in the present moment can often be missed when we're too strongly focused on a particular outcome. This by itself is not particularly serious. But if one gets in the habit of focusing so strongly on what isn't there, to the exclusion of what is, it can become physically dangerous, as your mind is elsewhere and perhaps not prepared to respond quickly to the situation at hand.

✦

David: Any other favorite phrases?

Nancy: "Failing successfully" has been another pet idea. To be able to survive a risk, albeit awkwardly, is exhilarating—whether it's a physical risk, an aesthetic one, psychological/interpersonal, or other. It builds confidence to try again.

✦

David: How has your nomadic travel and teaching affected your sense of "home"?

1977 Coming to Northampton and Body-Mind Centering

At our Vermont Contact Conference during the summer of 1977, I was introduced to the work of Bonnie Bainbridge Cohen by Beth Goren, who was one of her early students. In her class, she guided us into the experience of our own anatomical structures, not only bones but also organs. It was fascinating work, clearly the tip of an iceberg. It turned out that Bonnie was relocating from NYC to Northampton/Amherst, Massachusetts, and setting up a school there. I was going to be touring with Steve et al. on the East Coast that fall and needed a base. Lisa Nelson, who by then had become involved in making *Contact Quarterly*, was also going to be in Northampton studying with Bonnie. So I took a room in a rooming house there, taught a Contact class in her school, and began the immense experiential study of the body, through all the body systems, that Bonnie and her teachers were sharing. It has had a profound, subtle, and powerful influence on my perspective. ✦

NANCY AND LISA NELSON IN *DANCES BY HEART*, HARTFORD, CT, 1978.

Nancy: Often over the years I've felt I was "home" when I was in the same room as my dancing pals, my next of skin—more so even than when I was in my own apartment. That sense of homecoming seems to have less to do with geography than with people.

✦

David: Initiations in Improvisation—any metaphors, especially visceral, like "I wanna go home; my tummy hurts"?

Nancy: The human organism is a tender beast that opens to mean "yes" and shrinks to mean "no," amoeba-like. This is clear info for me. I call it the "organism check." There are also other bases for decisions while improvising: musicality, timing, aesthetics, safety, the past, underlying intentions. Sometimes the tummy wants to go home but the heart wants to stay. It happens that organs differ.

SUSAN SCHELL AT THE A CAPPELLA MOTION WORKSHOP, SMITH COLLEGE CREW HOUSE, NORTHAMPTON, MA, SUMMER 1985.

Nancy and Karen Nelson were going to do a performance at Thorne's in Northampton, Mass., in 1988–89, called *Everything Must Go*. They asked if I might come to some of the rehearsals to watch and give feedback. I was delighted. I had just given birth to my first child a few months before, and it would be one of few reentries into the world beyond my infant son. I was relieved to find it was still there and every bit as compelling.

I remember the first time I came—while watching, as my senses became increasingly engaged in the process, I became aware of a growing desire to draw what I was seeing. As I was drawing, the image of an hourglass/conduit started forming in my mind. All this life was going on out in the space, then funneling into my body, squeezing through me—out my fingers, the pencil, the chalk—and spreading back out on the page in a much abbreviated, graphic form. I was dancing; that's what I was looking for.

(continued)

✦

David: Do you have flashes/moments/memories from past dances that you carry close to your surface, as might occur in dreams or conversation?

Nancy: Yes, and dances in dreams that could never happen but live in my sensation as if I've danced them (flying, impossible landings, positions, timings). The world made and understood by dancing feels as illusive/elusive as a dream and as real as tying a shoe. How can it be so both at once? And yes, "memory does play a part" (Paxton, *Chute* video)—muscle memories; what has been seen, done, imagined—all inform current dancing decisions.

✦

David: In what way(s) has Buddhist meditation influenced your dance?

Nancy: The first summer after meeting Steve Paxton in 1972 and beginning to do Contact Improvisation, I was at his farm in northern Vermont. I think I asked him about concentration, staying focused on one thing. He gave me a lovely but ordinary smooth, gray stone and suggested I sit quietly and meditate on it. "What am I supposed to be looking at?"

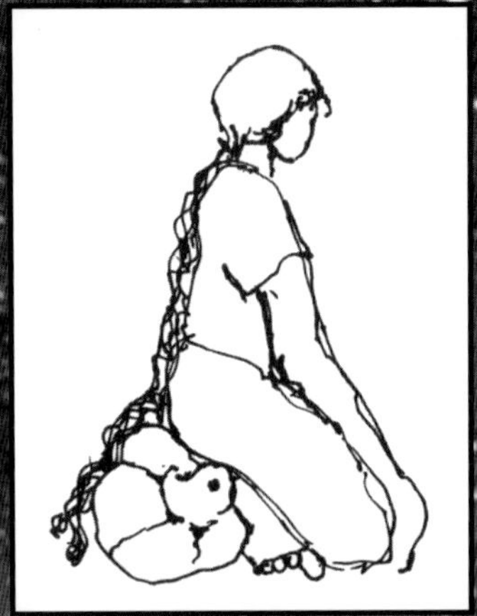

DRAWINGS BY SUSAN SCHELL OF NANCY AND KAREN IN REHEARSAL FOR *EVERYTHING MUST GO* WITH KAREN NELSON, NORTHAMPTON, MA, 1989.

(continued)

I began wondering, how many times before had I watched Nancy and Karen dancing—together, alone, with others? How often had I danced with them, together, alone? Enough to feel their bodies kinesthetically in my own as I was watching and drawing, enough to taste their weight in my bones. Often they would move so fast—a rhythm/pattern in their movement would just start to register in my body, and I would begin to draw and then the whole thing would shift to something else. A stillness would start having a certain mass for me and I would start to draw, never knowing how long I might have. I was having to leave many moments before I was finished filling them in on the page until what was not finished was becoming most satisfying. I became excited by putting as little on the page as possible while still revealing the dance. Sometimes what would end up on the page was much more essence than form, their signatures in movement, always forged through my perception and sometimes illegible to anyone but me.

I have probably drawn Nancy dancing more than I have drawn anyone else. Enough so that now, sometimes when I'm just doodling, I will draw a line and her body will suddenly travel through it and I will recognize it as the angle of her wrist when she is moving in a certain way with a particular energy. I am fascinated by how other people's dancing bodies live within our own, how they seem to be encoded in our organism and therefore somehow always dancing with us.

Susan Schell
dancer, colleague, friend
Chesterville, ME

I asked, a bit confused. "What exactly? For how long? Any other instructions? Just sit and look at this ordinary stone?" My Buddhist name, given to me by Tibetan Buddhist teacher Chögyam Trungpa Rinpoche in 1978, means "Dharma Joy of Patience." Ha! Sure, I thought. This must be what I'm supposed to grow into, not what I'm starting with.

Buddhist sitting meditation is a precious jewel—witnessing the complexity of mind—*pshew*!—glimpsing space, peace, emptiness. It's amazing to experience the enormous thrust and insistence of every little thought to exist and at the same time glimpse its insubstantiality. My practice, though continuous over the years, has been very spotty. However, the principles and practices of the teachings continue to deeply influence my thinking and experiencing of the world. I have great respect for this body of knowledge, enough to say I've only barely entered its rich domain. But a little can go a long way. It's had an enormous impact on me.

Another important principle from my Tibetan Buddhist (Kaygu lineage) studies

1979 Writing/Healing/Dancing

When I was at college, perhaps in an effort to figure out my major, I made a little diagram of the three things that were most important to me: movement/dance, writing, helping people/healing. By the end of the 1970s, I noticed that all three were coming together. Dance classes had burgeoned, touring had increased, the newsletter grew, and now we were making a special issue of our dance magazine, *Contact Quarterly*, on healing. ✦

BRIDGET ROSE SVANE O'HAIRE ON HER FIRST DAY OUT IN THE WORLD, WITH MOTHER CHRISTINA SVANE, IN AMSTERDAM, HOLLAND, 1990.

has been the pairing of intellectual study and experiential practice in the development of one's knowledge. Experiential and conceptual study. The first public talk I went to by Trungpa Rinpoche, though entertaining, felt a bit vacuous to me. Once I started to meditate, I began to perceive more of the substance in his words as it related to my own experience. Likewise, new concepts learned from reading and discussing the Buddhist texts deepened and strengthened my meditation practice. I have gravitated to this approach with dancing—enjoying both the doing and the studying/reflecting/talking/listening/articulating. They feed each other.

✦

David: When did you first encounter tai chi?

Nancy: Tai chi practice began for me around the same time as Buddhist practice, also at Naropa Institute in the mid-1970s, with various teachers—all first-generation students of Professor Cheng Man-ch'ing, mostly Americans.

The principle and experience of *chi* running through my body; the concept of "filling and emptying" weight into and out of legs by shifting weight, and being able to fill and empty partially, in percentages (for instance, 70% in front leg, 30% in back leg), were impressive and directly applicable to teaching/practicing Contact Improvisation. The only difference was

Mid-1970s Early touring buddies

Singing in cars was definitely part of our early training. We often made up songs on tour; like once, with ReUnion in California, each of the four of us contributed a line, with a change of scale for each phrase; a bizarre off-key-sounding song resulted, which turned into a round. It was called "Everybody's Buddies in Utah" and went like this:

Everybody's buddies in Utah,
They wear their friendship with a smile.
All across the width and breath of Utah;
Mile after mile after mile.

In the round, the "mile after mile after mile" would morph into "My laughter my laughter mile." Then we'd get out of the car somewhere, put our bags where we were staying, and go warm up and do Contact Improvisation. ✦

BONNIE BAINBRIDGE COHEN *[LEFT]* AND SIMONE FORTI IN THE BACKSEAT OF THE CAR, BOULDER, CO, 1984.

that in Contact the surface of the body touching the floor that was filling or emptying could be anywhere on one's body, not just your feet or legs; you might be inverted, on your shoulders, head, side, feet.

Also significant was the concept of moving from one's center, or *tan t'ien*, and the difference a small reorganization of the skeleton and shape of the body can have in the flow or obstruction of flow of chi. Also the power of light touch. Many things—most of them directly applicable to dancing—though, like meditation, I find it important to regularly practice it in its own "pure" form.

✦

David: The same for Contact? Is there a pure form?

Nancy: I guess I do feel the same about Contact Improvisation. Though no official "pure form," exists, it seems that CI jamming can reinforce CI's basic principles, creating a foundation, deepening

1980 A home base and expanding spheres of activity

31 Elizabeth Street was my first real apartment on my own, a home base in Northampton, Massachusetts, where people could come and stay over, have dinner, talk until all hours of the night, and where I was eventually evicted with a note that cited "all those strange artists carrying on up there." I loved the postman for Elizabeth Street. He started noticing all the interesting mail coming there for *Contact Quarterly* from around the world and asked if I collected stamps. For the next fifteen years, I kept a small box to share foreign stamps with him, ripping some off for him and keeping boxes of them for us. We now have many check boxes full of stamps and still collect them at *CQ*. For many years after I left Elizabeth Street, Larry the postman would forward my mail from there to the *CQ* post office box. I love living in a small town. ✦

NANCY AND CURT SIDDALL PERFORMING WITH REUNION AT THE SAN FRANCISCO MUSEUM OF MODERN ART, 1976.

its root, for whatever other use or application down the line. Of course it might also be useful to focus and refresh one's practice through study and consideration of the fundamental principles.

✦

David: A question about the hieroglyphs. The more I've looked into your hieroglyphs, the more fascinated I've become. Their shape, their change, their movement—will you cast some light on them?

Nancy: Dance in translation. A hieroglyph is a glyph, a written movement—not a drawing, but a written language based on tracking the rhythm of energy vibrating inside the body at that moment. It's a kind of EEG hookup, a 2–10 second dance on paper, in place, moving across the page in units, along a self-selected pathway—mine have tended to go from right to left. I've used hieroglyphs in teaching as a bridge between dancing and writing about dancing—to get over the sense of distance, difference, obstruction, intimidation dancers often feel about writing, especially about their dancing experience. I've found it fascinating to see how the forms that people's hieroglyphs take make sense in relation to their personality, their aesthetic, and their dancing.

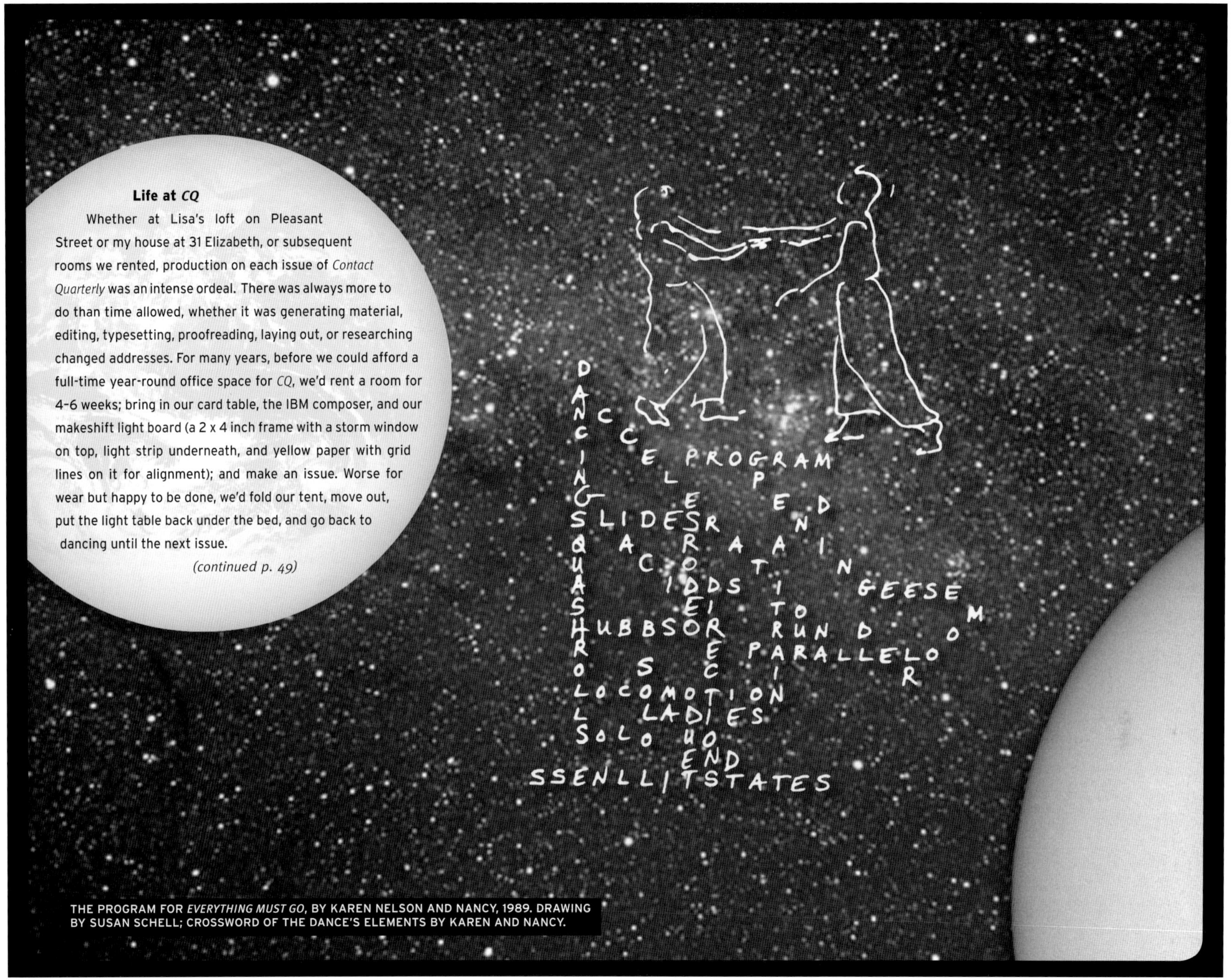

Life at *CQ*

Whether at Lisa's loft on Pleasant Street or my house at 31 Elizabeth, or subsequent rooms we rented, production on each issue of *Contact Quarterly* was an intense ordeal. There was always more to do than time allowed, whether it was generating material, editing, typesetting, proofreading, laying out, or researching changed addresses. For many years, before we could afford a full-time year-round office space for *CQ*, we'd rent a room for 4–6 weeks; bring in our card table, the IBM composer, and our makeshift light board (a 2 x 4 inch frame with a storm window on top, light strip underneath, and yellow paper with grid lines on it for alignment); and make an issue. Worse for wear but happy to be done, we'd fold our tent, move out, put the light table back under the bed, and go back to dancing until the next issue.

(continued p. 49)

THE PROGRAM FOR *EVERYTHING MUST GO*, BY KAREN NELSON AND NANCY, 1989. DRAWING BY SUSAN SCHELL; CROSSWORD OF THE DANCE'S ELEMENTS BY KAREN AND NANCY.

David: **What are scores? They seem to conflict with Contact principles?**

Nancy: Contact Improvisation *is* a score, a focus, a set of parameters for improvising. A score is a game plan, a set of instructions/rules/limits/considerations/foci, an operating manual, software for an improvised activity. These structures can predetermine time considerations (how long, when) and space (where, how to consider it); can specify activity, relationships, personnel (how many people? who?), what to focus perceptions on, image, particulars of body use, relationship to sound/music. If a score is not outwardly stated, each improviser will inevitably work from the operating manual of his or her previous experiences or make up a focus or have it shaped by present desire/circumstances. All of the above happens.

I often think of Contact Improvisation

One spring in the mid-1980s at Naropa Institute in Boulder, Colorado, Nancy taught a class on Friday afternoons that was composed of the three other classes she taught throughout the week. The range of experience in those classes went from people who had never ever done any Contact Improvisation to those who had had some experience, a lot of experience, and a group of internationally traveling performers. Fifty people in the class. When Nancy entered the auditorium, we were sitting, standing, leaning, stretching, chatting, and lying down. It looked like a cross-section of society had been dressed up in dance clothes and deposited in a large room for no apparent reason. The only thing similar about everyone was that they all looked uncomfortable.

Coming into the room, Nancy remarked on the size of the class and expressed thanks that the movable dividing wall had been opened to allow space for everyone. Then she asked everyone to crowd into one side of the room up against the wall. With so many people, there were about three or four rows crowded together all facing the opposite wall.

Nancy then asked us to all walk across the hall, but first wait until everyone was ready. Wait, lean toward the opposite wall, and all take off together to walk across the room. The first time, fifty individuals stepped off by themselves—bumping, bobbing, tripping, and crashing into each other and, finally, the opposite wall. The second time, the first row and part of the second moved together. The third time more. And by the fifth pass across the room, we all sensed something in each of us, and moved as if one.

Bill Arnold
photographer, friend
Florence, MA

BILL ARNOLD SELF-PORTRAIT AT ARLEQUI RETREAT CENTER, NORTHERN SPAIN, 1987.

as a score that Steve Paxton proposed in 1972. It has a predetermined focus. Dancers play out the score in the present moment however they might. Contacters have spent the last thirty-five-plus years investigating, playing with, unfolding the possibilities of this score and applying their findings in various contexts. But remarkably, the basic score seems to remain the same. Otherwise, I suppose one should call the activity something else.

✦

David: What does it mean "to inhabit the body"?

Nancy: For me, inhabiting my body is about feeling the actual sensations of my exact body in this exact moment—for example, expansion and release of chest with breathing, crick in the left trapezius muscle. It's about being present throughout your body as it is, not just having one to carry you around.

Present in the mass/matter.

✦

David: Is this what you mean by "body time"? How do you get there?

Life at *CQ* *(continued)*

CQ has always relied on volunteers, including Lisa and me. Whoever was around would help, and though Lisa and I did 99 percent of the work of making the magazine, we'd try to think of and thank every person who brought us a cup of coffee or answered the phone. It was somehow important to think of our effort as part of a larger vision. Mail and orders were taken care of by a stream of individuals over the years, first unpaid friends, then part-time dancers and artists who always put more into the organization than they took out: Paula's plaid pants and funny collages! Lisa Enzer's upbeat seasonal notes written to would-be advertisers! Hillary's heartfelt beseeching phone calls to deadbeat account receivables explaining that we were such a small organization and needed them to pay up and how could they... Jamie's hysterically dry humor, Mette's calm clarity and her dog friends that would accompany her to work, Harriett's detailed notes posted around the office about how things worked (how to print both sides of the page on the xerox machine, which way to load paper into the fax machine, etc.), Inga and Kendra's gallery of postcard images from the mail. And John, who was with us for over fifteen years, quietly keeping the office functioning, from the days when Lisa and I would fill the room with cigarette smoke as we cranked out issue after issue, with all the boxes of back issues labeled and lined up in three tiers of shelves around the room. What he had to put up with! And there have been many more saviors of *CQ* since then. ✦

"SILVER BULLETS," OR "PASS THE ANGEL," IN NANCY'S CONTACT CLASS AT NAROPA INSTITUTE, BOULDER, CO, SUMMER 1985. (BILL ARNOLD PHOTOGRAPHING IN UPPER LEFT CORNER.)

Nancy: Yes; being present in the body. How to get there? I focus my attention on my physical sensations—feel my weight in the chair, the stretch of a particular muscle, the action in my joints, the touch of the floor, clothes, movement. I synchronize body (sensation) and mind (attention). "Body time" tends to have a mutable, subjective aspect to it, which doesn't always correspond to the clock—some "minutes" seemingly long and spacious, while others go by imperceptibly fast.

✦

David: Do you have a primary notion of your relationship to floor or ground?

Nancy: For me, a complete relaxation/surrender of weight and tone into the earth seems primary (Tonic Labyrinthian Reflex). It creates a deep sense of security and a foundation from which to draw strength when pushing and extending the support through the body as one's level rises. It's also useful to learn how to make

NANCY AND NIECE JULIE BERENZWEIG IN A QUIET MOMENT AFTER ROLLING AROUND ON THE FLOOR, 1985.

NANCY AND NIECE JULIE AT A FAMILY GATHERING AT THE HOME OF GRANDFATHER "PAPA JOE" SMITH ON LONG ISLAND, NY, c. 1992.

1982 ***Fade In, Fade Away***

One summer, Steve and I made a performance at Naropa called *Fade In, Fade Away*.

Our preparation was writing short pieces about some very specific aspect of the other. He wrote about the inside of my Datsun King Cab truck and how I arrive and leave places. He wrote about my close relationship with Ernestine, a housekeeper that mothered me early on. I wrote about how he eats his toast with breakfast, stacking it up along the side of his plate; how he looks rocking in his chair at the farm while making a decision; and how the back of his neck resembles his father's. We read the short pieces into a tape recorder, which played while we were doing Contact.

For that same performance, we also wrote out a long list, each of us separately, of things that we were thinking about, or aware of, when doing Contact. Then we read them into the tape recorder, taking turns, then overlapping, in a kind of chant: "I'm thinking about my partner's bones, my partner's hair, my partner's weight"; "I'm thinking about my partner's rings, my partner's timing, my partner's humor"; and so on. I think we called this section DanceTalk, and it began with the audience asking questions that we'd answer as we danced. Then we'd say, "Any more questions?" and the tape said, "I have a question. What are you thinking about when you're dancing?" And then the prerecorded litany of considerations would play while we continued dancing. I remember feeling transparent as we danced, like the audience had been given a way to see not only the outer form of our dancing but an x-ray of what we were thinking as we moved. I loved that way of offering some of the dimensionality of the dancing experience through performance. I also really enjoyed writing those small vignettes about tiny and particular aspects of Steve that I had come to know from working and living around him. ✦

smooth transitions through the last six inches down to the floor and up from the floor, so you're not afraid of falling. I also find it useful to try to balance the force of gravity with the force of levity.

✦

David: Expound a bit on the phrase I've heard you say: "Tension masks sensation."

Nancy: Steve Paxton used to say this regularly while leading the "small dance." I quote him often because I find this principle simple and key. If, for instance, your arm muscles are contracted and tight, the sensation of tension will overwhelm more subtle sensations, such as the weight of your arm (gravity). In the same way, excess muscle tension elsewhere in the body will mask other sensations, including the small movements that your body is executing to keep you balanced. It's useful to be sensitive to this subtle activity so that the play between the body and the physical forces can be more articulate, complex, and dimensional.

It's sometimes necessary to release excess tension physically and mentally—to relax—in order to be available to perceive subtle info being transmitted by the environment or from our dance partner. On the other hand, it's possible to be too relaxed, with not enough tone (Paxton: "Relaxed is almost right, but flaccid is

Male domesticity and the secret sauce

I have an image of Steve sewing before many performances, often very complicated little bags with flaps and pockets that he had designed—a kind of Rubik's Cube type of origami pouch. In my nervousness before performances, I couldn't imagine settling down to sew, and I wondered if it relaxed him.

Many of the men I spent time with during my twenties and thirties taught me domestic skills that I missed growing up mostly without a mother. Steve's little sewing projects and various cooking projects (stuffed green peppers in Oberlin, pies of all sorts in Vermont) and thorough cleanings (of floors mostly) were instructive. I got the knack for barbecuing from my father, whose regular stints at the grill when I was little would draw all the neighborhood kids for what he called "tasters." He had a "special sauce," also known as the "secret sauce" that he said you had to marry into the family to get. Our neighbor once tried to steal it by coming over during the day when my father was at work and saying he had permission to get the recipe. But he didn't get the secret instructions with it, and his chicken was charcoaled on the outside and bloody on the inside. I remember my father getting distinct pleasure from the neighbor's failed attempt. ✦

NITA LITTLE CATCHES NANCY IN REUNION'S PERFORMANCE AT THE SAN FRANCISCO MUSEUM OF MODERN ART, 1976.

wrong," *Chute* video). This principle applies to our mental condition as well. "Not too hard, not too soft." That's a tai chi principle.

✦

David: Intimacy varies with the individual's experience and relationship to personal and social norms. Touch itself, except clinical touch, is still often taboo. Part of the gift—the grace—of CI is to offer experiences of different kinds of intimacy in a safe environment.

Eavesdropped on a Wednesday evening Eugene CI jam: "It's the intimacy part that frightens me." "That's not an issue for me; I just stay unattached."

Nancy: The experience of intimacy does seem to occur between partners in CI with more or less regularity and intensity. It depends on the temperament of the dancers and the circumstance.

I wonder: Is intimacy social? Is it personal? Transpersonal? Can I have it with

When you were in college, I loved to listen to you talk and to read what you wrote, your ideas and thoughts like slow-flying birds, or grass growing, breaking the ground softly. I used to think then that the beauty of how you thought had to do with your life at school. But I know now that it was simply you, it was how you were born into the world, strong and searching.

A few days ago I found your old postcards, all faded, dusty and beat up. And so full of happy affection, always reminding me that some day you would drive up in my yard again like a gypsy woman, your house on your back. Oberlin was a homey pit stop for you, I imagined. But for me our roles were reversed: it was you who made a bed and laid a table in my life. You gifted me.

Remember that Walt Disney rainbow? It was a sad, angry time in my life. You drove in at the finish of a fine August thundershower and a big powerful rainbow stood over us. It seemed near enough for us to climb a tree and touch it. Climbing out of the car, you smiled and called out, "We've been following this rainbow and it ends at your house, M.P.!" Right away, my heart stood up, and I remember I felt smoothed out and happy because you called me back to consciousness of the things I love. You can always turn me like that.

With love,
your old M.P.
"M.P." Jean Binford
catalog librarian (retired)
Oberlin College
college landlady, friend
Oberlin, OH

"M.P." JEAN BINFORD, CATALOG LIBRARIAN AT OBERLIN COLLEGE, EX-LANDLADY, FRIEND, OBERLIN, OH, 1980.

anyone? Everyone? Are there moral issues involved? Emotional? Social? Does my experience of intimacy depend on my partner's? Does the future have anything to do with it? Intention? Are there energetic/emotional laws that govern the experience of intimacy just as the physical laws of gravity and inertia govern our motion? Are there things to help one prepare to ride those forces safely, just as falling practices keep safe our physical frolic? Probably yes. All of the above.

✦

David: What is "dancing with heart"? Can you speak about the "emotional body" in your movement?

Nancy: It's one of many "bodies" moving inside the dancing. It gets stimulated, surfaces, hides, colors the movement, may or may not have noticeable content, weaves up and under other threads in the dancing fabric. I used to think that emotional response was just raw energy to be put back into the physical dancing. I still think that, but now I am also noticing and enjoying more of its specific nature and color and texture as it rises and falls and intermingles with the other aspects.

✦

LUCY, NANCY'S MOTHER, GOOFING AROUND ON ASSIGNMENT FOR "TIME OUT" PUBLICATION, c. 1943.

SUSAN AUGUSTA SMITH BERENZWEIG, NANCY'S SISTER, SUMMER 1991.

LUCY WRITING OUTSIDE AT THE COUNTRY HOUSE OF A FRIEND, c. 1947.

Working with Steve

Early on in our Contact touring, Steve got a summer teaching residency at American University in Washington, D.C., and invited me to join him. "This is not a help-Steve position," he wrote in the letter. This was a real sharing of responsibility. (He even shared his full teaching fee 50-50 with me!) This kind of casual assumption of equality extended by Steve occurred throughout that first decade of working together—so much so that I didn't realize until much later that he had indeed been a most important teacher for me. I learned sideways from him, as co-pilots, deeply internalizing both his thought processes and his body's sequencing from literally dancing up against his body (and mind) for so many years. Even now, he comes to mind often, and not just when I'm "quoting" him while teaching. Regularly I'll find myself holding a mental or aesthetic decision up against my sense of him and seeing what kind of reflection I get, influencing, one way or another, what I end up doing. ✦

David: Over the years, what doubts or apprehensions have you felt about your work and/or life?

Nancy: That it, the work, fills the frame of my life too fully. That its metaphors of life become my life. That my life becomes too self-referential, work centric, that I see life too completely through the work's lens.

✦

David: Airplanes and travel—how do you do it?

Nancy: Going where the dance is makes it worth it. It's often not until I'm actually in the studio dancing that it makes sense for me to have traveled there; that's when I feel oriented. At this point in my life there are friends, familiarity, favorite restaurants, views, markets, homes in many ports. I sometimes get the feeling of being reeled in from one "home" to the next.

SIMONE FORTI IN PERFORMANCE AT NAROPA INSTITUTE, BOULDER, CO, 1984.

It's also enjoyable for me because being in the airport marks the successful completion of that fierce, rigorous process of finishing projects and preparing last details before departure. That adds to the free-floating feeling.

✦

David: Dietary evolution since leaving home? Unique foods in specific locales: Spain, Italy, Indonesia, Japan?

Nancy: I saw a zucchini for the first time in college. I had many vegetable firsts then, including how a pumpkin becomes a pumpkin pie. Miracle! And eating tasty fresh green salads, mmm. Not until my twenties did I discover the ecstasy of eating what you or your friends grow outside; that's the ultimate pleasure.

I've been introduced to many new tastes, textures, flavors, from world travels—a sweet, black Chinese soup of rubbery ligaments of something; a fabulous cold Chinese drink like apple cider but of some wonderful smoky aromatic tree bark; the clean feeling of the Japanese diet—breakfast of rice, miso soup, pickled vegetables; and fabulous noodle soup stocks; special Austrian pumpkin seed oil on salads; Catalan grilled bread rubbed with fresh tomato and sprinkled with olive oil, salt, and pepper...

Love and work

By the end of my twenties I began to recognize that I wasn't in a long-term committed relationship with one person but with a whole body of work and the other people in it. It was a family of sorts, and home was wherever we were, whether in Vermont, Massachusetts, New York, California, or Europe. ✦

NECA ZARVOS AND NANCY PERFORMING AT A MUSEUM IN SÃO PAULO, BRAZIL, 1993.

✦

David: How did high school prepare you for this profession? What is this profession?

Nancy: To love moving—through sports and gymnastics; to love rigor, teamwork, breathing hard, communication, good leadership. High school also offered me ecstatic singing experiences—a cappella choir and madrigal groups, Vivaldi's *Gloria*—inspiration, hard work, detail. I loved learning languages and doing creative writing. There was a lot of academic rigor, which I also enjoyed: learning how to concentrate, work through a difficult problem, and get the job done. My father was quite the academic-high-standards stickler: "98% on the test? What happened to the other two points?" he'd say playfully, but he meant it.

Watering holes, ports of call, annual events

In looking back, I see that I had established quite a regular annual circulation between several regular ports of call throughout the 1980s and into the '90s. The structure of the year was organized around the production periods for *Contact Quarterly*. When I wasn't making the magazine, I was dancing. I lived in the work, in the associations through the work—in the markets in Amsterdam; at a special lookout spot up Flagstaff Mountain over Boulder; in the meadow pools at Breitenbush Hot Springs in Oregon; in the airports smoking cigarettes (until '86) and doing crossword puzzles with friends on the road. Every year there'd be some new places thrown in amid the regulars as the dancing circles expanded, later including annual workshops at Arlequi in Spain and the Bates Dance Festival in Maine—more homes away from home for the work and me, each with their favorite spots and extended family of colleagues. ✦

WATERCOLOR BY LISA LEIZMAN OF THE CREW HOUSE STUDIO AT SMITH COLLEGE IN NORTHAMPTON, MA, WHERE THE A CAPPELLA MOTION WORKSHOP WAS HELD EACH SUMMER FROM 1981 TO 1996.

✦

David: How has your love of language led you? Prominent poets and persons of words in your life?

Nancy: From an early age, I sensed the power of words to communicate and affect personal reality. I think my earliest journals and diaries were as much prayers as documents of the day's activities and feelings. Later, I saw how writing could be not only a way to communicate something already conceived, but also an important part of the process of bringing the ineffable not only to language but to consciousness in the first place; to bring language to meet real experience, and vice versa. Articulation. Documentation. Poetry.

In leading dance classes, I began to notice how words not only influenced the students' understanding but acted as catalysts effecting real physical/energetic changes in their movement and mind state. The power of a word or image, formed and delivered at a particular time in a particular way, was magical in its effect. Words as drugs for changing states. So language cannot only describe but also *induce* dancing states. This isn't always the intention of the words but is often their effect.

NANCY AND ANDREW HARWOOD *[OFF THE GROUND]* PERFORMING AT THE A CAPPELLA MOTION FACULTY CONCERT. *[BEHIND, LEFT TO RIGHT]* DANIEL LEPKOFF, JULYEN HAMILTON, SUSAN SCHELL, NORTHAMPTON, MA, 1985.

SNDO

The School for New Dance Development in Amsterdam became an important destination on the "new dance" map throughout the 1980s. I went there first with Freelance (Steve, Lisa Nelson, Daniel Lepkoff, Christina Svane, and I), a company of people who had been dancing together for most of the past decade. We were on a European tour and did a residency at SNDO that included a lively array of classes from Contact Improvisation to Special Studies, in which anything might happen—including, in one of Steve's classes, a comprehensive lecture demonstration on how to take care of your feet, including the art of decallusing the feet with a butter knife. At the end of the residency, we were feted in the top floor chapel studio by all the students and teachers and were each given an almost human-size chocolate bunny (it must have been near Easter). All of us continued to come back to SNDO many times over the years. Meetings with other artists teaching at the school were fertile, and I always looked forward to whatever surprising mix of artists might be there on each visit. The students were eager and creative, many of them now spread all over the world, teaching, performing, and heading up "new dance" programs and studios in many countries. ✦

At Naropa Institute's first summer session in 1974, I studied poetry with Diane di Prima, Allen Ginsberg, and others—bold, honest Buddhists writing of real life in contemporary language, respectful of their predecessors; well-read and high-visioned. Diane's offer to apprentice her brought me to California, where I continued to study writing with her and to learn how to typeset and layout small press publications.

✦

David: Historical points where your dance took relative tangential turns or your vocabulary expanded noticeably?

Nancy: After years of sports, gymnastics, and a spot of modern dance training, I got to work with Twyla Tharp and her company for a month while a student at Oberlin College. Oh! I realized, dance can be interesting, physically rigorous, full-bodied, quirky, thoughtful, athletic, smart, clever, and use more of me, with a greater

1981–96 A Cappella Motion

Every year for two weeks, usually in June, at the Smith College facilities in Northampton, Mass., I would be at A Cappella Motion, our annual "state of the work" exchange and workshop, produced by a small collective of teachers and sponsored by Contact Collaborations, our nonprofit parent organization. Our days and evenings were chockful of classes, jams, faculty and student performances, discussions, singing, video. One of the main reasons we kept the workshop going was the opportunity to dance in the gorgeous old all-wood Crew House dance studio, with three sides of screenless windows out to Paradise Pond, rowboats housed in the water under the dance floor, and that smell of old musty wooden camp lodges, lying on the floor stretching and watching the reflection of the water dance over the ceiling, swatting the mosquitos during each hot evening's performance. We were always amused at the timing of the inevitable pronouncement from the bullfrog across the street during performances. A Cappella was a major annual touchstone—between teachers as well as the remarkable participants who came from around the world. It ran every summer for sixteen years. ✦

PARTICIPANTS AT CI25, THE 25TH ANNIVERSARY CELEBRATION FOR CONTACT IMPROVISATION, OBERLIN COLLEGE, OBERLIN, OH, JUNE 1997.

variety of kinds of movement than I thought. I loved it. This really was the moment I turned my love of movement in the direction of dance.

After seeing me in Twyla's residency, dance teacher and company director Brenda Way invited me to join the Oberlin Modern Dance Company, and I entered a few years of classical modern (Graham, Humphrey) and contemporary modern (Hawkins et al.) training in the daily company class and began making pieces.

Brenda was a mover and a shaker and an inspiration to me. I was thrilled to join her and others (mostly Oberlin dance students) in the summer of 1972 for three months in the Martha's Vineyard woods (in Mass.), living in tents and dancing daily on our outdoor dance floor—training and making work. (And going to the bars at night to dance to the jukebox and meet the local folks.) It was a dream come true but also painful when we realized that we weren't all headed in the same direction. I realized by contrast how deeply committed I already was to improvisation. We were called the Oberlin Dance Collective, a group that Brenda later reformed and took to San Francisco.

For the January 1972 Winter Term project after Twyla, Brenda invited the Grand Union, an avant-garde dance theater improvisation company from New York, to come for the monthlong residency at Oberlin, in which I participated. The Grand Union was

STEVE PAXTON TEACHING AT CI25, OBERLIN COLLEGE, OBERLIN, OH, JUNE 1997.

JAMMING AT CI25'S MIXED ABILITY WEEKEND, OBERLIN, OH, JUNE 1997.

STEVE PAXTON'S CLASS AT CI25, OBERLIN, OH, JUNE 1997.

Breitenbush Contact Jam

For more than a decade, the Breitenbush Contact Jam, produced by Joint Forces and held during the early spring at the Breitenbush mineral hot springs resort in the Oregon mountains, was an annual event for me. I served in an evolving series of roles, first teaching a short morning class and doing some afternoon individual sessions, then being part of the "small brains group" that would help keep discussions focused and organize the post-jam performances, until by the end I was just one of the dancers hanging around—soaking, dancing, watching, talking, steaming, performing, napping. Breitenbush was another one of my important dance watering holes of the year: a regathering of the extended dance family, catching up on lives and dances and ideas. ✦

an improvisational dance theater company in the early 1970s made up of Yvonne Rainer, Steve Paxton, Barbara Dilley, Douglas Dunn, David Gordon, Trisha Brown, Nancy Lewis, and others, who had been pushing the boundaries of dance since their Judson Church Dance Theater work in New York City in the mid-1960s (a revolutionary period for dance in which they were central players). Another total mind and body swerve. Yikes: Yvonne Rainer's pedestrian movement and complex art mind; Barbara Dilley's "personal warm-up" and eight-hour mandala walk/performance/event around the field house that cold January; Steve Paxton's 7 a.m. "Soft Class" of breathing, standing, balancing, "small dance"ing, "smallest stretch"ing, noticing the dawn; David Gordon's *Sleepwalking* piece with marching legs, "surrender" hands, getting shot against the wall and dying, being reborn or dreaming it. (I remember having trouble keeping track of the steps David showed us because I became so hypnotized watching his feet—every day in another fabulous pair of high boots, clicking his heels perfectly, precisely, like

Dharma dancing

Summer visits and occasional school-year residencies at Naropa Institute in Boulder, Colorado, were a regular and significant part of my year throughout my twenties, thirties, and beyond. The glorious backdrop of the eastern slope of the Rockies was present at all times, the days hot and dry, the skies blue blue blue, rainstorms most late afternoons, cool evenings, the smell of sage present on every walk, growing wild on every path. I still go back irregularly, and even as it expands, changes shape and personnel, I always feel that I've come home when I drive into Naropa's parking lot—to reconnect with friends and mountains and immerse myself in the mix of contemplative practice and art in Naropa's ever-evolving manifestation.

Naropa was another major meeting point, with many opportunities to collaborate with respected dance colleagues—Barbara Dilley, Ruth Zaporah, Simone Forti, Bob Dunn, and poets and musicians. Naropa helped me stay connected with meditation practice and dharma teachings through its remarkable summer spectrum of teachers like Chögyam Trungpa Rinpoche; His Holiness the Karmapa; Khyentse Rinpoche; and many Zen teachers, including Maezumi Roshi and Kobun Chino Roshi. A very precious time.

We offered some great combo workshops during those summers at Naropa: I did one with friend and colleague Richard Heckler—black belt aikidoist, psychophysical researcher and teacher, author, and bodyworker—focusing on physical and psychological states of body/mind. Every time we'd move together, I'd instinctively connect my center to his and he'd instinctively try to throw me down. Another time, Steve and I and tai chi teachers Jane and Bataan Faigao combined tai chi and Contact, doing "push hands" together late into the night at their house, like physical chess. ✦

BILL T. JONES AND NANCY, SKIDMORE COLLEGE SUMMER DANCE PROGRAM, SARATOGA SPRINGS, NY, 1998.

a Gestapo, as he showed us the choreography.)

And then there was Steve's men's piece, *Magnesium*. They used the ancient, dusty, canvas men's wrestling mat to practice rolling, soft jumps and collisions, and slides and falls, and also practiced the "small dance" of standing—"the extremes of orientation and disorientation," as Steve later referred to the piece. The performance took place in Warner Gym, a shiplike wooden gymnasium at Oberlin, with the audience watching from the running track above the gym. The men began standing for several minutes and, during the fifteen- to twenty-minute piece, spilled out of their standing into a profusion of staggering, falling, jumping, rolling men, erupting and colliding and spilling softly yet with great energy and physicality through the space, alone and with whomever they encountered. The piece ended with five more minutes of standing. I found the physical fountaining of men extraordinarily beautiful. I was so moved that I mentioned to Steve that I'd love to know if he ever worked this way with women. A few months later, he invited me to be part of the first performances of Contact Improvisation.

This whole downtown New York post-Judson explosion of dance forms and ideas was very new and exciting to me. Their work and stance—current, disarmingly honest, primitive yet sophisticated, intelligent, actively exploring new territory—was fascinating and attractive.

Bill

The serendipity of *CQ* renting space in his factory building brought me into my first real live-in personal relationship with photographer Bill Arnold, who taught me not only how to live with someone but how to delight in what I saw. Before being with Bill I didn't really understand what people meant when they talked about conflicts between their personal life and their work life. I guess to me they had been so interwoven that I never felt any conflict. Even though Bill and I were often engaged in each other's work, I was beginning to understand the dilemma of trying to find time for a personal life. I didn't realize I wasn't really having one before, and now there wasn't enough time for everything. How do you separate one from the other? Where do you put everything? These questions were woven through the six fertile and enjoyable years of our living and traveling together, and they continue to be central in my life. ✦

NANCY AT BOROBUDUR TEMPLE IN JAVA, INDONESIA, DURING THE TRIANGLE ARTS PROGRAM, OCTOBER 1997.

David: Other practices and people of influence?

Nancy: Another significant line into my dancing has been tai chi since 1976, which I still practice every morning (boy, do I need correction!). Also a little aikido—enough to appreciate those precious pure forms and principles in my body and mind. Eastern martial arts have generally been a huge resource. The sense of center and initiating movement from there; identification of the idea of *chi*, life energy flow—why don't WE have a word for that in our language? Steve used to regularly note with incredulity that we have no word in the English language for the shift of weight from one leg to the other.

And then of course there has been Steve Paxton, his dancing mind and body, a main-line long-term infusion into my dance veins for many years.

Quitting smoking

Thanks to Bill's support, I quit smoking on January 28, 1986, which turned out to be the day that I was interviewing Bonnie Cohen and also the day the space shuttle Challenger blew up. Quitting smoking opened up a deep, raw emotional flow that I hadn't realized was constricted; it introduced me to a sadness I didn't know I had and taught me how to tolerate my own tears. It was tremendously empowering to be able to give up a pleasurable but enslaving addiction. ✦

TEACHING AT A CAPPELLA MOTION WORKSHOP, NORTHAMPTON, MA, SUMMER 1985.

Years of contact with Bonnie Bainbridge Cohen and her Body-Mind Centering work has been hugely influential, both in taking classes and in working with her on *CQ* articles and interviews—turning me on to the minds of my body, how all of them—every system, organ, tissue, cell!—are alive and can speak, receive and transmit, support and initiate.

Later and continuously, dance artist Simone Forti's simplicity and purity of form and concept have been an inspiration and reference for me. Her ability to look at something that doesn't have a name, that's in the process of forming—dance, art, poetry—and conceive of it in a delightful new way is remarkable; I admire it tremendously. I learn a lot from Simone and enjoy spending time with her in many ways.

Working with dancer, choreographer, thinker, improvising performer extraordinaire Lisa Nelson on the making of *CQ* for thirty years has been a huge part of my life and work. Her artistic brilliance, her penetrating intelligence, and her unique and mysterious views have been deeply informing for me. Our collaboration has helped me sharpen my own articulation and thinking. The simple fact of our having coproduced this opus of thirty years of magazines, with all its challenges and satisfactions, is staggering and bewildering! We are a most unlikely match, and I've learned a lot from our differences and our common, relentless passion for the work we do.

ALAN PTASHEK AND NANCY PERFORMING AT "CONTACT AT 10TH AND 2ND," THE 11TH ANNIVERSARY OF CONTACT IMPROVISATION, ST. MARK'S CHURCH, NYC, 1983.

Volleyball

My local coed volleyball team became another kind of family for me over the years and a good physical balance to the dancing. Our team slowly formed through YMCA pickup games and included lawyers, economics professors, bank presidents, electricians, machinists, painters, and pastors—citizens of my town that I might not otherwise know. After years of getting to know each other, they started to get used to my physicality, my handstands and elaborate falls and rolls, and even my jumping up against them. "You look better missing the ball than anyone else I know," they often said.

This volleyball community was a casual but deep commitment and throughline in my movement and social life locally: weathering the literal and figurative ups and downs of team sports; seeing each other week after week (for 15+ years); showing up on the court through times of sickness, some of our numbers dying, marrying, having children; children growing up and going to college; a small encyclopedia of phrases accumulating over the years coined by one or another teammate, used with humor and heart twinges; my bad habit of not moving instantly to the setter's spot after the ball is served so I'm always racing late to where the pass goes in order to set it. In typical New England style, we played for many years before we ever saw each other off the court, but it turned out we were there for each other when we needed it. ✦

There are, of course, many more colleagues, students (*extremely* important and influential!), friends, and folk in the world whose ideas and practices and presence have informed, influenced, and inspired me.

Most recently, the music and mind of composer and improviser Mike Vargas have contributed enormously to my thinking and practice—illuminating the relationship between composition and improvisation; the power of art; and the value and beauty of silence, empty space, and humility.

But has my dancing changed dramatically over the years? Taken "tangential turns" or my "vocabulary expanded noticeably?" With a few exceptions (Tharp, Grand Union, Contact), I don't see that as clearly. For the most part, it feels more like a slow evolution than major gear shifting.

✦

David: What is this idea called the Pathway of Movement—that which connects and dissolves the dots...

1990 Vast interiors

In the summer of 1990, after more than six years of living and traveling together, my relationship with Bill Arnold ended suddenly with a phone call. I was at Naropa in Boulder, he in Amsterdam, and on the phone he said that he was with another woman now. Though I was aware of problems in the relationship, this solution was, to put it mildly, a surprise to me.

Seeking sanctuary, I went up to Mad Brook Farm where Steve Paxton, Lisa Nelson, and Simone Forti lived. I remember Steve talking about the "vast interiors" of great artists like Maria Callas and Alec Guinness, and I felt met in my sorrow by the idea that these vast interiors might have been excavated by pain. One thing I realized as I experienced the raging heat through my heart and veins on those first days and months of heartbreak was that my broken heart was also an open heart, and though it was painful, it also felt good, and I felt connected to a powerful, vital, emotional, sexy life force that deepened and dazzled me. I realized that the more I was able to embrace my own pain, the more able I would be to tolerate that of others. I came to understand that my natural cheerfulness would only be a half happiness if I couldn't also experience pain. Believe me, I wouldn't have brought this on myself, but there's no doubt that it has been a necessary and desirable gift. ✦

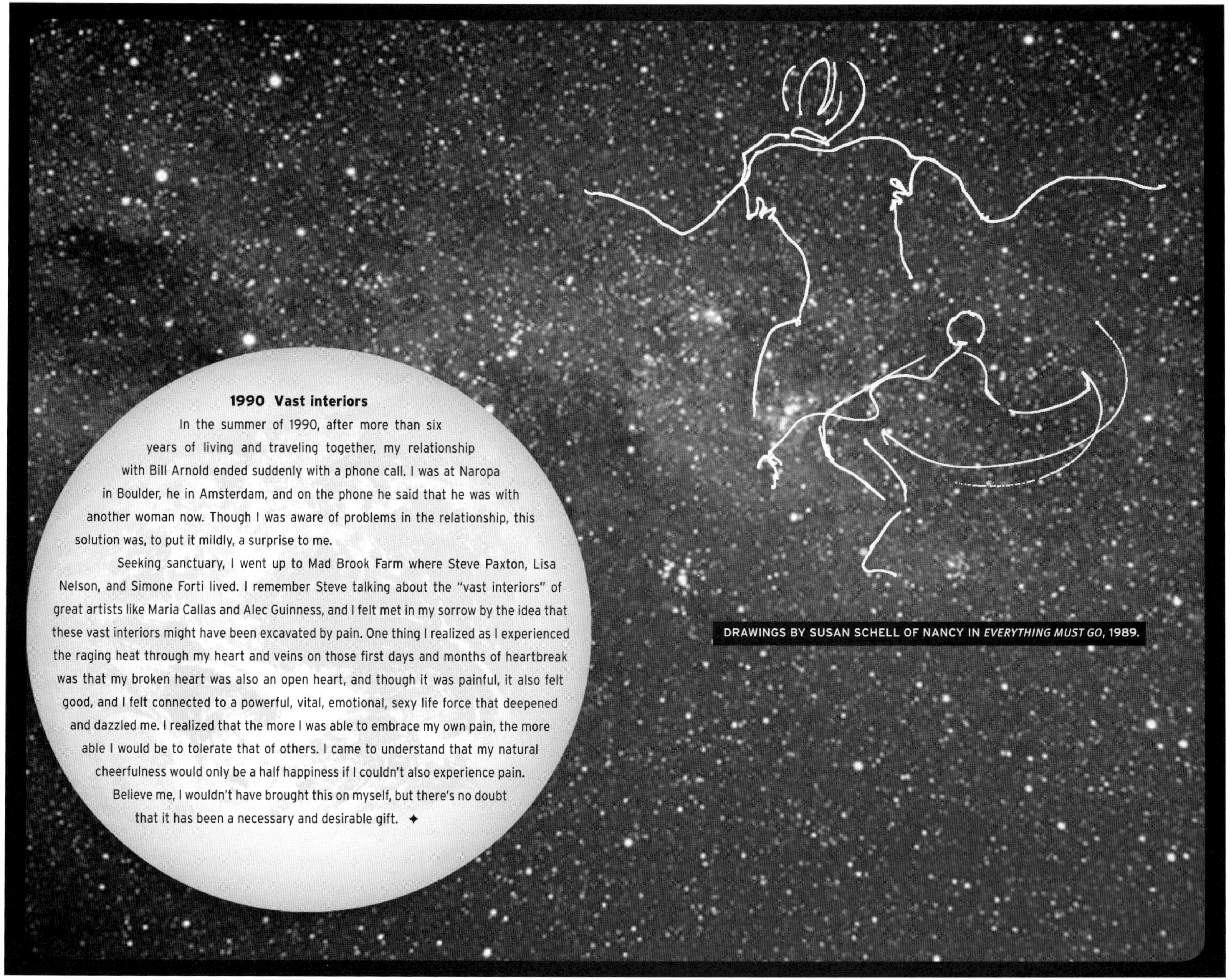

DRAWINGS BY SUSAN SCHELL OF NANCY IN *EVERYTHING MUST GO*, 1989.

Nancy: Flow—the sense of an ongoing stream of movement, both individually and also between partners; a continuity.

Like in playing music, where you first learn how to blow or bow an instrument and then you learn how to do half notes and quarter notes and as you get more familiar with your instrument, you can articulate different-sized elements... In a similar way, "flow" in Contact Improvisation creates a kind of baseline of operation between partners. It's a basic hum, the continuous blended flow of weight in movement and balance that we can connect with through touch and where we can find each other physically. (This connection is also a safety feature; it links your awareness and your partner's; any change in the flow will be communicated instantly to both of you at once, so you can get a first alert and be ready to act.)

Once you establish clear flow, you can toy with the basic hum as you like: impede it, redirect it, play it, subdivide it. It's a place where you can meet and communicate with your partner, feeling and enjoying the flow through and around the endless "obstacles" that arise. That was one of your definitions of Contact wasn't it?

✦

[LEFT TO RIGHT] BILL YOUNG AND MARTIN KEOGH AT AN OUTDOOR ROUND-ROBIN AT CI25, OBERLIN, OH, JUNE 1997.

TOM GIEBINK [ON SKATES], ALITO ALESSI, BRUCE CURTIS [IN CHAIR], AND OTHERS IN THE MIXED ABILITY PERFORMANCE AT CI25, OBERLIN, OH, JUNE 1997.

ANDREW HARWOOD [ABOVE] AND NANCY PERFORMING AT THE SCHOOL FOR NEW DANCE DEVELOPMENT, AMSTERDAM, HOLLAND, 1985.

David: "Contact Improvisation is the natural flow of obstacles."

Nancy: Yeah; more and more, physical flow seems to simply be a model for (and training in) the continuity of attention.

✦

David: In verbal communication, intention is always at play: the difference between what is expressed and what is understood. How is this applicable to CI?

Nancy: In Contact Improvisation, we're moving right up against our partner's skin. Initiations and responses are all interwoven. This can make it challenging to sort out what's coming from you or from a synergy between the two. The difference between what is expressed and what is understood is always complex in any communication, CI

JULYEN HAMILTON AND NANCY PLAYING AROUND ON A TRAMPOLINE IN BOULDER, CO, 1985.

included. It could be that I suddenly get very athletic in a dance, or in another moment I feel, for whatever reason, that my heart can fly open. I don't know that this means anything outside of the dancing. It's true that intention is strongly communicated through the dancing, subtly or otherwise. How we interpret what we receive has a lot to do with our own intentions. In Contact Improvisation I feel that I must always stay tuned in to the pure physicality—no matter what emotion is going on. That's my intention.

✦

David: Some would have us believe that a child receives parents' unfulfilled desires/expectations and goes forth to complete them. You think?

Nancy: I don't know...but my father (doctor, teacher, former athlete) did seem to take some pleasure in my dancing the few times he saw me. I think he knew how right it was for me, was silently proud of the magazine, but still hoped I would "stop this peripatetic lifestyle" and settle down. Become a doctor? Marry one? In his last years, he showed me the melancholy poems he'd been writing for some time.

My mother, Lucille Deborah Stark—Lucy, Starkie—was a writer for *Life* magazine, a researcher who went spelunking and to debutante balls for the "*Life* Goes to a Party" column. She lit up the room, so they say. She didn't make it past

I first met Nancy under a full moon in July 1974. She picked me up at the Denver, Colorado, airport; I was arriving for my first teaching gig at the new Naropa Institute (now University) in Boulder. She was studying with Diane di Prima and other poets that summer of Naropa's beginning. We connected again later that year near Stinson Beach, California. All these connecting points over the years have been filled with rich, deep conversing. This particular way of talking makes many of those times clear memories for me. I remember lying around on the floor of her house in Northampton, Massachusetts, and lying around on the floor of my house on 41st Street here in Boulder. Dates don't seem important; rather the sense of the continuity of the conversing, the mode of diving into our lives, the willingness to find language for often hard-to-speak experiences. And to this day, whenever we get a chance, we pick up the threads of our exchange, and the conversation runs along like a clear stream in the soft light of evening, without any drying up.

Barbara Dilley
dancer/colleague, friend
Boulder, CO

BARBARA DILLEY PERFORMING AT NAROPA INSTITUTE, BOULDER, CO, SUMMER 1984.

thirty-five. It seems that I've carried some of her pleasure in play, language, and people.

✦

David: How has your concept of love evolved?

Nancy: Backwards. I'm still getting there. I wonder about the relationship between transpersonal and personal love. I am regularly filled with tears of joy and compassion from the former, but have only come to know the latter more recently. It's still evolving.

✦

David: If at first you don't succeed, try less?

Nancy: Often during "the stand," the "small dance," Steve would say, "Can you feel less?" directing our attention to smaller and smaller units of stimulation and change within our

Da Costakade, Amsterdam. In the spirit of *Raku*, you perform, as I witness. Through my "outside eyes," I saw a piece evoking, among other things, the timeless mystical world of the fetus. We discover moving manifestations of the lightly formed woman emerging from the girl-child.

Running backwards, you passed a gymnast, a shaman, and a soul not afraid of heights. Slowly, with trust, you developed honest material, inching toward extreme states—physicalizing growing up before growing older.

I feel strongly that part of what we did together was to probe the taboo of improv being once and once only. By maintaining creative and sometimes inspired rehearsals, we could both develop material and set or score some places and points to return to. You kept humor and spontaneity. I worked to bring it over time—to evoke, impact, and effect, not once, but performance after performance.

Jenn Ben Yakov
theater maker, friend
Amsterdam

1990–91 Finding *Raku* 1

In my discomfort during the first days and weeks back home in Northampton after my breakup with Bill, I felt a strong desire to go alone to a small studio nearby and just be there. Most of the time I just lay still, breathing, looking out the window sideways at the rain, at the clouds. Sometimes a deep breath would release, maybe a sound would come out with it, maybe a song, again a welling of sadness, some tears.

After a few weeks of almost daily visits to the studio, I began to notice something. In my attempts to get some relief from the uncomfortable burning sensation in my body, I would adjust my sitting or lying position to accommodate what felt like a very heavy and bruised heart area, one that felt not only actually sore but extremely hot, radiating in thin vein-like channels of lava through my arms and into and around my pelvis and legs. As the lava would start to flow inside me, it would ask that I move my body a tiny bit this way or that to allow the passage of the flow through some joint or tissue; then maybe another adjustment farther down the arm—rotating the forearm a few degrees, bending the wrist, extending or folding the fingers just so; or a suggestion inside my body to balance the accumulating organization with a softening of weight in the opposite right hip, and then the head turning a tad to open the flow through the neck. It was all very very small, probably imperceptible from the outside and done only in an effort to tolerate, to relieve, my feeling of pain and discomfort. Periodically, after several little adjustments, I would suddenly feel perfectly balanced, organized, at peace, not needing to move any more. I would hang out in the stillness, energy raging through my still form, until the raging came to rest and the instruction to change position would occur again. I didn't even wonder what any of this was; if it helped me feel a little better, it was very attractive. *(continued)*

NSS LETTING DOWN ON THE OVERNIGHT TRAIN BETWEEN WORKSHOPS IN SPAIN AND AMSTERDAM, 1987.

physical circumstance. This heightened sensitivity reveals a universe of subtle sensations—of your own body's movements and those of your partners—the timing of tiny shifts of weight, arm hairs passing across your forehead—ecstatic, informing, amusing. This awareness of subtlety helps make the changing condition of the body, as it ages or experiences disabilities or obstacles, an opportunity for new directions.

✦

David: Focus on your collaboratory process for creating dance/work/material.

Nancy: Improvising in performance with others is one form of collaboration I am most familiar with and on which I was kind of raised. I spent many hours in my early performance life watching the Grand Union create and destroy their temporary forms of dance and theater throughout an evening's performance. I loved watching these life forms build and topple, studying the behavior, marveling at the forms and circumstances that accumulated and how they were managed.

My experience of collaboration has sometimes been of a conversational sort, like in CI—a back and forth, an offering and responding and counteroffering of material with another artist, developing, over time, some territory

Finding *Raku 2* *[continued]*

I spent a few months mourning and going to the studio and making the magazine in Vermont until it was time for a little performance series in which I needed to show something. No way would I be able to "bounce back," to reinhabit my perky little throw-myself-around-the-space kind of solo dancing, falling and flying and rolling and rising with gleeful abandon. Not a chance. But what could I show? The only thing I'd been really doing with my body was this microshifting heartbreak dance. Could I really show that?

My respected colleague and friend Simone Forti was also performing on the program, and I asked her if she would come and look at what I was thinking of presenting and give me some feedback. I did the slow movement but then accelerated it toward the end until I was moving in a more "normal" tempo with some of my usual dips and dives. When I was finished, Simone nodded many times with her head cocked to the side and in her inimitable way said, "Yes, yes... I could have watched that slow section for *much* longer. And that section where you're moving faster, I'm not quite sure what you're doing there." She had nailed me.

She went on to talk about how she was seeing Buckminster Fuller's lines of *tensegrity* in the lines of tension and connection from inside my slow moving form out through the whole space. Well, of course, that's because it was Simone looking at it, but her comments gave me enough courage to show what came to be named *Raku* (for a form of pottery made by exposing the clay to intense heat all of a sudden, and admired for its cracks). This was the beginning of a long slow development. Even after my own personal heartbreak had healed, often when I'm doing *Raku* I know I'm on the right track if I feel a profound sadness tapped, a vulnerability and strength that goes backwards and forward in time and is no longer just mine. And I can feel when I'm not there, when I'm approximating it. ✦

NANCY PERFORMING *RAKU* AT AN A CAPPELLA MOTION FACULTY PERFORMANCE, SMITH COLLEGE CREW HOUSE, NORTHAMPTON, MA, 1996. SET: JONATHAN KOHRMAN.

together.

I have also experienced a more synergistic model in which the combination of the two minds focusing together has created a kind of harmonic, an "other" coming from the two. I have often quoted writer William Burroughs in his statement about collaborating with a visual artist on a book, that whenever two minds are collaborating, a "third mind" is at work. Robert Ellis Dunn referred to this phenomenon as "the unicorn." I've also thought of CI duets in this way, as having many moments in which this third mind was operating. But the third mind only operates when the other two are turned on. It's not about passivity and divine intervention.

✦

David: What about Group 6?

Nancy: Working with Group 6 was another sort of collaboration—six improvising dancers, usually two improvising musicians, evolving a

Peripatetic lifestyle

My habit of being away from home is long-standing—sleepaway camp from the age of six, avoiding tensions at home by preferring to be in the apple tree in the backyard or off riding my bike, at intramural sports, or at a friend's house.

Over the years, as my touring schedule showed no sign of slowing down, my father's oft-repeated line when picking me up from the airport or visiting around his kitchen table was, "When are you going to stop this peripatetic lifestyle?" It became something of a joke, but he never stopped asking for the next twenty years. ✦

CHRISTINA SVANE, *DANSPEECH*, 1987.

process for making improvised dance performance. The group was a vehicle for our study and practice of improvisation in performance, specifically integrating Contact Improvisation with other forms of movement improvisation and other compositional concerns not usually focused on in pure CI practice.

I enjoyed the collaboration with Group 6 very much (dancers Peter Bingham, Ray Chung, Chris Aiken, Julie Carr, Jeff Bliss, and me, and musicians Coat Cook and Ron Samworth). The constancy of the group's members allowed the work to substantially deepen and move forward at each meeting. It gave me an opportunity to dance, study, and perform in ways I love with others who share an enjoyment of the physicality along with intelligent dialogue about ideas, desires, and methods for working with improvisation in performance. It was also a group of people who were good at communicating and taking responsibility, and who wanted to continue to learn and develop.

Group 6 evolved a clear framework for working: warming up solo and with Contact Improvisation (and watching); isolating specific "studies" to practice (for example, strengthening solos, starting the group improvisations from particular forms in the space, trying different relations with the music); and then doing an open set for a period of time, evaluating it, and coming up with studies and issues for the next day's practice. Our studies informed the mostly

1994 A home of my own

One rainy November, with much trepidation and indecision, I purchased my first home. My father had indoctrinated me into believing that I needed a solid brick house, already in good shape, that I would just have to maintain. But in the end I bought the shabby (but lovable) little rental cottage on the outskirts of town that I had been renting for several years. It was a dump, with no direct heat on the second floor, two porches that were rotting, old push-button electric outlets that were dangerous, and what I had always thought to be a dirt basement but that actually turned out to be a concrete slab covered with several inches of floodplain from the driveway runoff that would break into the basement window. In other words, a headache. But I loved it there and I decided to stay.

In all the years of traveling, throughout all my "peripatetic lifestyle" wanderings, there were many people and places that I loved and where I felt at home. But to have my own home, to be at home there, to always be welcome, touched me deeply. Less than a year later, my father (who had raised me largely as a single parent and was still the only person who was always tracking me) fell ill suddenly, a week after his eightieth birthday. At that time he was still getting up at dawn, going to the medical school to do rounds and teach. When I got the call to come down to New York, that he might not make it through the night, and I closed the door behind me to drive the four hours from Massachusetts to the hospital where he was, I said out loud to my house, "I'll be back." It gave me great comfort to know it would be waiting there for me when I returned, with or without my father still alive. ✦

MEDITATING IN BOULDER, CO, c. 1977.

open sets we did in performance.

Over about four years (in the mid-1990s), each of the six of us produced a residency for the group in our hometown (we were spread across the U.S. and Canada). Following our most satisfying performances, recognizing that our geographic differences and growing family commitments were becoming more and more difficult to surmount, we disbanded on a high note. Members of the group continue to work together in various combinations.

✦

David: What is a "studio visit"?

Nancy: Going into the studio with an artist friend (working in any medium) to have a "visit" by sharing the space for a period of time, each person going into his or her work state alone, with permission not to interact—no, the *rule* is not to interact. The emphasis is on co-existing—the other's presence and focus and engagement with his or her own work acting

Sometime after I got to know you, I found out that you were born the same year that I was, and I was excited, as I don't know very many people born the same year as me, let alone one who does CI. I've felt a certain affinity with you because of this, being born in the year of the dragon, and a water dragon at that. Every twelve years the Chinese astrological signs cycle through one of the five elements: metal, water, wood, earth, fire. This inspired a poem.

Silvery haired water dragon lady
Slipping through the streams of dancing bodies
On her journey 'round the orb of humanity
Gradually beginning to know her own secrets
When will you find your much sought treasure?

It's short, but from a man of few words, it's a lot.

love,

Ray Chung
dancer, colleague, scientist, friend
San Francisco, CA

GROUP 6 REHEARSING AT SALLY NASH'S WORKSPACE FOR CHOREOGRAPHERS, SPERRYVILLE, VIRGINIA, 1995. *[PICTURED, LEFT TO RIGHT]* CHRIS AIKEN, PETER BINGHAM, NSS; *[NOT PICTURED]* RAY CHUNG, JULIE CARR, JEFF BLISS.

as a kind of environmental/energetic ballast, leverage, encouragement, for the other to do the same.

Perhaps because of so many years doing Contact Improvisation, I found that my tendency in most situations was to adapt my behavior to harmonize or somehow relate to others in an environment. So I made this studio visit form to practice staying focused on my own work while enjoying the presence and concentration of my friend in his or her own work/world. Occasionally the works might find an unexpected and surprising meeting ground. It is also a desirable way to be together, intimately, with friends without talking. Simone Forti named it after a "visit" we had in Vermont.

✦

David: And now, more recently, with Mike Vargas?

Nancy: Mike Vargas, composer and improviser, and I have been collaborating since 1998—he on piano, percussion, and other instruments; me dancing. The solo dance framework has allowed me to pursue my own idiosyncratic conceptions and practices in conjunction with another artist, composer, improviser who has a vast, different but compatible set of tools, concerns, and intentions. Generally we bring our own forms and structures to the table and see which ones work well together, experimenting with different

CASINA SETTARTE DANCE RETREAT CENTER IN CISTERNINO, ITALY (IN THE HEEL OF THE BOOT OF ITALY), AFTER A STORM, DURING A WORKSHOP BY NANCY AND MIKE VARGAS, 2003.

TYPICAL "TRULLI" HOUSES IN THE APUGLIA REGION SURROUNDING CASINA SETTARTE.

levels of structure and varying relationships between the music and movement. (We have also worked with several short-term ensembles and work groups.)

This meeting of minds and media allows and, in fact, forces me to clarify and expose my own particular solo dancing mind in a way that Contact Improvisation and other ensemble dance improvisation hasn't quite done. I see how they all feed and inform each other.

We've also been teaching together quite a bit, developing new ways to link composition and improvisational practice, to develop listening skills in the dancers, and to explore the many relationships between the dancing and the music. Mike's extreme intelligence and constant reading, listening, thinking, and innovating have been an education and an inspiration to me.

✦

David: How did working solo feel after so much Contact?

1998 The big round Earth

In the 1990s, my touring began to take me further afield, and I popped into the Southern and Eastern Hemispheres for the first time. I remember the funny feeling of leading a "small dance" in New Zealand and asking the students to face the direction of their birthplace (assisted by my pocket compass). This is an exercise in connecting one's position in the studio to the larger map (as best you can picture it) and zooming out, imagining where you are relative to somewhere else—it could be your birthplace, or where you are going after the workshop, or some special spot on the premises, or some other direction I might give—and turning to face it. I was born in Brooklyn, NY, and I was greatly amused to realize that day in New Zealand that not only could I just as well face left or right, but the closest way might be to look straight down! In that moment, I really felt like I lived on the globe, an inhabitant of the big round Earth. ✦

NANCY AND MIKE VARGAS *[ON PIANO]* PERFORMING ***ASTERISK*** (*), CENTER FOR THE ARTS, NORTHAMPTON, MA, 2001.

Nancy: When I first started exploring solo work in earnest after decades of doing Contact Improvisation and other ensemble work, I remember having the feeling of somehow "getting away" with something. For the first time, I didn't need to negotiate, didn't have to make my choices understandable, decipherable, manageable, respondable to by a partner; the logic could be purely my own for that moment. I have to admit that although I love collaborating and moving forward by bouncing ideas off others, the relatively unconditional experience of the solo statement is a tremendous relief.

✦

David: What is wanting in your present life/ career?

Nancy: Time: for everything!—dancing, gardening, love, writing, projects, home, family, friends, being in nature, contemplative practice, learning new things, research, performance making, seeing art, reading. I could use a more gracious, expansive, yet incisive management of time. I'd like to make a few books—one about Contact that would be a compilation of teaching methods and essays from many CI teachers and practitioners; maybe one of photos I've been taking over the last ten years. And always, there's room for more humor.

"TALK-BUBBLE" DRAWING BY MIKE VARGAS.

MIKE VARGAS, COAST OF MAINE, 2001.

✦

David: Aging, maturing, and refining? Gross matter and subtle matter?

Nancy: I am inspired and encouraged by older dancers continuing to develop their dancing and their work, and I hope to do the same. (*Am* doing the same!) I sense that my intelligence, wisdom, and imagination continue to develop as does body refinement. I am also beginning to experience aging creating new limitations. Societal pressures and prejudices about aging bodies (and about dance) can make the going more challenging. But I sense that in our time, more of us will be finding ways of continuing our dancing work well into our maturity/seniority. The potential for refinement is great—I'm enjoying it. Meanwhile, I have to say I've been very lucky with my body—no serious illnesses or injuries.

NANCY AND RUTH ZAPORAH WALKING IN THE ROCKY MOUNTAINS DURING A SUMMER WORKSHOP AT NAROPA INSTITUTE, BOULDER, CO, 1986.

For my 55th birthday, Nancy went up to Tilden Park, a wild and gorgeous expanse that stretches along the top of the hills of Berkeley. She collected fifty long and graceful yarrow sticks, which she later presented to me along with a copy of the *I Ching*. Then she taught me how to throw the sticks to receive the wisdom of the oracle. Even though I haven't used them since, over a decade later, I keep them out and pass by them all the time. When I do, I think of Nancy, a sort of sister, and of our way together, which is one long forever conversation about improvisation.

Ruth Zaporah
Action Theater founder, colleague, friend
Santa Fe, NM

But I feel my body changing, no question about it. I think it might be more articulate than it was, and I can still access the rowdiness and still love it when I get to it, but it's not the same body/mind as a twenty-year-old jock, athlete, dancer person who just can't get enough physicality, just loves eating it up, you know, burning it up. I still love that state when I get to it, still have a strong appetite for it, but it lives among other choices of focus and qualities of interaction. I have more access to and interest in subtlety than ever before, more interest in art—and a greater need for a good warm-up and excellent bodyworkers in the nearby area!

✦

David: Has the CI focus changed significantly over the decades since its beginning?

Nancy: I think the essence has remained the same—communication between dancers through touch, weight, balance, impulse, and movement, in partnership with the physical forces. A return to the physical forces as a major focus of the dancing conversation seems to be cyclic and important. The actual physical sequences and vocabularies (specific lifts, falls, ways of responding to certain physical overtures), styles (acrobatic, pedestrian, martial, mystical, dancerly), attitudes, and

DRAWING BY MIKE VARGAS.

CI25

We missed the twentieth anniversary of Contact Improvisation in 1992, waving to it as it went by. "We" being Contact Collaborations—a nonprofit entity formed in 1978 to umbrella *Contact Quarterly* and other new dance projects of interest to us—Steve Paxton, Lisa Nelson, Danny Lepkoff, me, and a few others who functioned largely in spirit only. So when the twenty-fifth anniversary arrived, a celebration was definitely in order. CI25, as the event was called, was one of the most ambitious and satisfying events I've ever put together. The devotion and creativity of the twenty-five curators and the many others who stepped in to help were inspiring and a lot of fun to be a part of. And the exalted feeling of dancing in Warner Gym at Oberlin again—that glorious wooden, ship-like studio, site of Steve's *Magnesium* in 1972, which I had seen as a student twenty-five years before and which changed the course of my life for good.

In addition to everything else that was going on, people invented spontaneous forms for celebrating. I loved the little "Small Dance Booth" that Karen Nelson made by the entrance to the old gym building. A folding partition marked off a small interior space, inside of which was a paper on the floor with outlines of footprints. Stand here. Do small dance. Draw outline of your feet (with awaiting marker pen).

The minute of silence that preceded each of our daily half-hour curator meetings was a sweet moment for me. I'd collect new agenda items quickly as people ran into the room for our noon meeting, all of us with our cold drinks and sandwiches, finishing conversations, rushing to get to the room on time from some other engagement. Meanwhile, all around us, people were jamming in the gym, taking class in the studio, reading someone's thesis in the reference room, looking at old photos and posters mounted and hanging along the walls, waking up with coffee and a conversation on the front steps, coming down the hall to xerox something... All in, we'd close the big wooden door to the corner library and start. With silence. Sixty seconds on the clock, simply being quiet together, the sounds of life all around our meeting room rising up as we settled down. Breathing, listening, thinking, not thinking, a minute passes and we turn to our agenda directly, efficiently solving today's little (and big) problems. The meeting ends and we're off, back into the fabulous fray. ✦

applications seem to grow and change over time and reflect current cultural issues. But I'm amazed how versatile CI has been, how it continues to have relevance as political and cultural agendas shift over the years. Whether Contact is used to spice up choreographic partnering or as a way for hundreds of people in Argentina to find positive community at a time of great political and economic crisis, somehow it all seems to be able to happen without threatening the integrity and clarity of the form's basic DNA. The basic dance form itself doesn't seem to change even as the times and styles and applications might.

✦

LUCY ON ASSIGNMENT FOR *LIFE* MAGAZINE, 1946.

MOCK *LIFE* MAGAZINE COVER MADE FOR LUCY WHEN SHE LEFT HER JOB THERE TO HAVE CHILDREN, 1948.

David: Let's parley about the playfulicious attitude in CI, okay?

Nancy: Yeah, sometimes I feel so darned serious: this is *such* fascinating, profound stuff. And then something in the dancing simply delights me—a ride, a timing, an unexpected turn that trips me up—and I'm completely happy. Play is good and can be weirdly wildly wonderfully complex and adult, and at the same time simply fun.

✦

David: Everything is speeding up—CI too?

Nancy: Well, it's spreading—does that mean it's slowing down because it's covering more global surface area? Or is it building momentum,

1997
Triangle Arts Program (TAP)

"I can't go; it's during *CQ* production," I said resignedly. "You *have to* go," Lisa insisted. Wisely. Created by a partnership of forward-thinking, generous arts organizations (the Asian Cultural Council and the New England Foundation for the Arts), the Triangle Arts Program turned out to be an incredible gift. One dancer and one dance producer/manager from the U.S., Indonesia, and Japan were invited to spend three months together, one month in each country. The six of us learned, shared what we had to offer, exchanged with one another in and out of the studio, and were exposed to a staggering richness of dance culture in each country through trusted and deeply knowledgeable guides.

For instance, Sal Murgiyanto, a beloved Javanese dancer, producer, and advocate of Indonesian dance, brought us through his country on a golden thread. We were welcomed into the home of Pak Sidja, a master Balinese mask dancer, who gave us a private performance with his son and home gamelan; we went to a large temple celebration and witnessed long lines of women arriving with skyscrapers of fruit and chickens on their heads as offerings; and we went to a dance school in Java, where we exchanged demonstrations with the students and received the special honor of a performance by Ben Suharto, an ailing yet still transcendent dancer of feminine roles in Javanese dance. And all of that might have happened in just two days! I filled two notebooks with writings from our three-month journey and took thirty rolls of film. It gave me a way to mark the enormous beauty and specific tastes of what I was experiencing; a way to say Yes, Yes, and this, Yes; Thank you, Yes. ✦

NSS IN SOLO PERFORMANCE, NORTHAMPTON, MA, EARLY 1994.

getting faster, going farther? *It*, Contact, seems to have changed not much at all; *we*, maybe, see/experience it differently. Time is definitely mutable in CI.

Contact does seem to have geographical high and low tides, meanwhile flowing into some unexpected niches—dancing with elders, disabled dancing populations, recreational "free dancers," dance therapists, and more and more traditional dance performers and educators. Overall, it's still growing: more of its ideas and experiences being tested, considered, practiced, applied, shared. It might be that one can learn the Contact form faster these days—it's more familiar; there are more techniques, exercises, and references to make it more easily accessible, and there are more jams available for practice with experienced dancers.

✦

David: CI25—WOW! Want to give it a nutshell whirl?

1998 D-Day

In the spring of '98, when I saw Mike Vargas's photo in the Bates Dance Festival brochure, I had a sudden jolt, a premonition that we might get together. I would be teaching there that summer, and he was coming as a musician. We had met four years earlier, performing together in Boulder at Naropa with dancer Jeff Bliss, an old friend and colleague of Mike's from their days in Liz Lerman's company in D.C. It was a wonderfully synchronous performance. I was single at that time and intrigued by Mike, but he was married. Oh well. End of story.

I must have heard that he was no longer married, and as much as I tried to get him out of my mind, he kept popping in that spring. Repeated lightning and thunder in the cabin at Earthdance where I was staying for a workshop only reinforced my heightened state. And then, when I got home from the workshop, there was a polite postcard from Mike (who I hadn't been in touch with since our performance) with a copy of his new CD, *Whispering the Turmoil Down*. More goosebumps. I responded with a postcard of a volcano erupting. "Funny, I was just thinking of you..."

When we got to Bates, I was expectant but reserved. And though we enjoyed long talks about art and improvisation, and performed in the festival's improvisation evening, he didn't seem particularly available or interested on a personal level. Meanwhile, just seeing his hand on the armrest of the theater seat where we often sat next to each other at festival performances made me swoon.

By the last day of classes, nothing had "happened," so I decided it was time to let go of the idea. I sang myself a little letting-go song as I swept the floor before my morning class. Good try; end of story.

We were both early for the final festival party; only the DJ was there. So we danced. I figured what the hell and just let myself have some fun. As any Contact-lover might, I danced near, up against, and bouncing off of Mike's body. Nothing personal, of course. "She tackled me on the dance floor," is how Mike tells it.

The floor was crowded with throbbing dancing bodies, including mine, when Mike came up to say he was leaving to drive back to Colorado. I walked him to his car, and we stood by the car talking, then leaned on the car talking, and finally were sitting on the hood of the car talking for hours. My sweaty dancing body eventually chilled in the August Maine night air, and with my teeth chattering, I innocently said, "I'm freezing!" He put his arm around me and, well, something changed. We call our anniversary D-Day because we left a permanent dent in the hood of his car. ✦

Nancy: CI25 = Contact Improvisation's 25th Anniversary Celebration in 1997—the largest, most complex, and most pleasurable event I ever produced. I worked with twenty-five "cocurators" around the world (early days of email made this possible) to create this two-week event at Oberlin College in Oberlin, Ohio.

CI25 included a three-day training intensive; a mixed-ability weekend; and a weeklong "Jubilee" of classes, performances, "small group" events, panels, "chat rooms," a photo and art gallery, a reference room of all manner of written/published material about Contact, a video library, and 24-hour-a-day jamming in the most exquisite studio—an old, all-wood, men's gymnasium (the site of *Magnesium*, Steve's men's piece that's considered the seminal work for Contact Improvisation).

Two hundred and fifty people from around the world attended, quite a few from the original CI event in 1972 as well as those entering the work at all periods until the present. It was a glorious occasion. The huge circles in Warner Gym felt as comfortable and intimate as a few old friends in a living room. Extraordinary. Generosity and appreciation were the main currencies. It was a positive, rigorous, pleasurable exchange on many levels of the work. From all signs, it was an event that uplifted and sent us forward with enthusiasm

Making work with Mike

Asterisk (*) is a duet that Mike and I have been developing and performing since 1998. You could say that it is a docking of two solo universes—a gentle collision that reveals a variety of human states within the play of predetermined forms. One strategy we've been finding fruitful in our collaboration is matching up compatible/resonant solo forms that we've been working with and letting them coexist side by side—each one with its own internal logic playing up against the other in unpredictable ways. One of the sections of *Asterisk* (*) is "Raku in the Wind," a marriage of *Raku*, my slow solo movement state, and *The Wind*, Mike's structured improvisation for solo piano with equal parts of playing and not playing. ✦

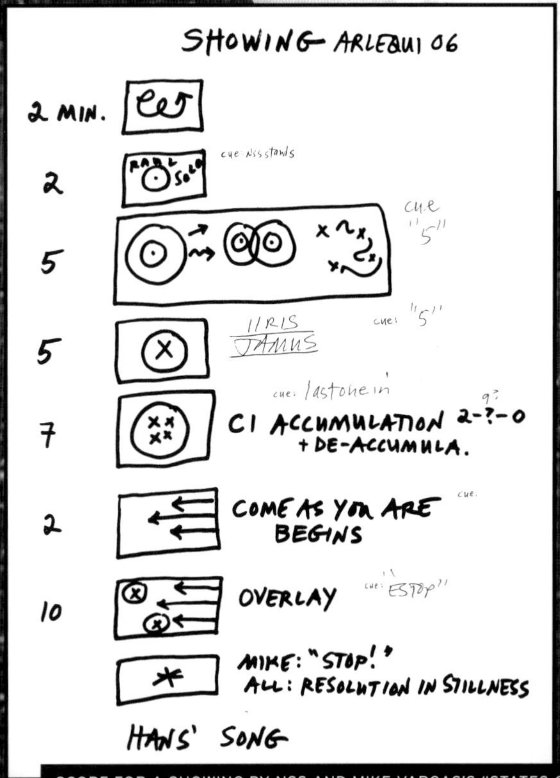

SCORE FOR A SHOWING BY NSS AND MIKE VARGAS'S "STATES OF GRACE" WORKSHOP AT ARLEQUI RETREAT CENTER, BANYOLES, SPAIN, 2006.

PETER BINGHAM AND NSS IN ***BASELINE***, A PERFORMANCE COLLABORATION WITH MIKE VARGAS (PIANO) AND JAMES PROUDFOOT (LIGHTS), AT EDAM, VANCOUVER, B.C., CANADA, DECEMBER 2004.

into the next "quarter."

The principles of CI were in clear operation daily in our organizational structures and behavior: cooperation, spontaneity, responsibility, intelligence, innovation/invention, sensing self and other, finding freedom inside limits, communication of support and change, enjoying the ups and downs, follow-through, and so on. I was proud of us, the work, and honored to be part of it all. Directing the event and co-curator team was like driving a golden chariot, and I am still glowing from the experiences there.

✦

David: It probably deserves its own separate book, but could you briefly outline that long score that you've been working with over the last decade or so?

2003 Casina Settarte and a surprise ending

It was the last day of our two-week workshop at Casina Settarte in the heel of the boot of Italy. It was an idyllic setting near ancient olive groves—each uniquely twisted tree looking like some sort of alien—with conical stone "hobbit" houses called "trulli" dotting the dry landscape. A breezy outdoor dance floor was open to the valley on three sides, with a large, woven tarp/cloth roof wafting in the breeze. Butterflies and friendly lizards crossed our path as we danced.

For our last class, Mike and I were planning a session of trio work that would end with an unannounced three-minute improvisation by each trio alone in the space. When we started the class, I explained the trio work and added that there'd be a surprise at the end.

During the session, the sky suddenly got dark, and the wind picked up and started thrashing the woven cloth roof like a ship's sails in troubled seas. And with thunder and lightning, it began to pour. We ran inside to a smaller indoor studio and went on with our now-miniaturized improvisations. As we neared the end of our session, the weather cleared, and when we ran outside to check the damage, we found two enormous full-arc rainbows filling the sky above us. "Is this the surprise you meant?" someone asked. ✦

NANCY AND FRANCO ZITA DANCING AT CASINA SETTARTE, CISTERNINO, ITALY, 2003; RAFAEL COHEN *[BEHIND, LEFT]* AND PAULO CINGOLANI LOOKING ON.

Nancy: The Underscore—yes, I'll try. It's a score I've been working with since 1990 as a dance improvisation research and practice score that prepares for and integrates Contact Improvisation within a more open structure for improvising.

The Underscore has several phases—moving from solo releasing/deepening into solo warm-up through space, Contact Improvisation, group improvisation, and back to rest and reflection, integrating CI into a broader field of improvisation and compositional dancing. Each phase has a symbol, and some have subsets. It is still developing in terms of its components, concept, and application.

In addition to being an intriguing tool for researching dance and improvisation phenomena, it's being used more widely in Contact Improvisation communities around the world as a way to focus and concentrate their jamming.

See the back of this book for descriptions of the Underscore phases.

✦

Summer 2005 Biggest Underscore yet

A recent Underscore phenomenon for me was offering the practice at the Freiburg Contact Festival in Germany for the full festival group of two-hundred-plus people. Though only seventy-five were in our intensive (!), I tried an experiment to see if we could get an Underscore off the ground with a large group of contacters with minimal preparation. I gave a two-hour talk-through the night before, detailing the phases. The next day we raised the two folding divider walls and began the *preambulation* in a space the size of a soccer field. Mike played live music with a borrowed keyboard, his Middle Eastern dumbek (drum), and assorted sound makers. As the dance progressed, it became almost overwhelmingly dense and complex, and I feared that we might lose the coherence of the score. Then, shortly after I called "*five minutes to final resolution*" throughout the giant gymnasium, one by one the dancing duos, solos, and groups arrived at stillness throughout the room. And as our city of dancers resolved in stillness, the church bells outside began to ring. ✦

BLURRY ROAD. PHOTO BY BILL ARNOLD.

David: Last words?

Nancy: 

✦

NANCY EMERGING FROM THE LAKE AT CAMP WOODLANDS, BRIDGTON, ME, 1961.

DAVID KOTEEN SURVEYING THE PAGES OF *CAUGHT FALLING* DURING A BOOK RETREAT WITH NANCY AND DESIGNER LILA HURWITZ ON VASHON ISLAND, WA, 2000.

2006 Return to Mad Brook and the shape of that mountain ridge

It had been several years since I'd made it up to Mad Brook Farm in northeast Vermont for a visit—a place that I used to consider another home, where I'd been coming to visit Steve Paxton, Lisa Nelson, Simone Forti, and others since I first met Steve in 1972. Site of many visits, romances, magazine productions, talks with Steve at the kitchen table—maybe a game of Chinese checkers, a good laugh, a pie—a walk up the hill with Simone or through the garden with Lisa. This time I slept in the living room of the "main house." Looking out the window from the main house, across the field, the view of the next mountain range is a perfect series of slopes, beautiful at any time of day in any kind of weather. Seeing the shape of that mountain ridge again made me want to weep. What could be in a shape that makes it so inspiring and so much like home, like love? ✦

David: Wait! There's yet time for a coupla more questions...

Sound of Nancy tackling David

✦

backwords

by Steve Paxton

photo: NSS

Steve Paxton on tour on the West Coast, 1975.

ohio

I met Nancy Stark Smith at Oberlin College, in Ohio, during a residency of the Grand Union—the anarchistic improvisational dance company—during the 1972 winter break between academic semesters. She had a car, which she generously used to ferry us around; Oberlin was a dry city in those days, and transport was needed outside city limits to find a beer.

She didn't attend my dance class, which was for men, but she did attend a 7:00 a.m. session I gave—consisting of deep breathing and some yoga—and ferried her friend Eleanor Huston, who was on crutches at that time, as well.

The prototype for Contact Improvisation, *Magnesium*, was created there, and after its performance, Nancy told me that if it was performed again, she would like to be in it. I was startled. It had not occurred to me that such a rough-and-tumble dance would be of interest to a woman.

new york

So when in the spring of 1972 I wanted to show a version of this new sort of improvisational work in New York City, I asked Nancy as well as the men who had performed *Magnesium*, plus other young athletic dancers—men and women—from the University of Rochester and Bennington College, as well as friends from the downtown dance scene in New York. The videographer of *Magnesium*, Steve Christiansen, was present to document the weeklong performance—"Contact Improvisations"—at the John Weber Gallery.

california

I got a chance to examine these videotapes in another Ohio moment later that year, and Nancy watched them with me. We began to bond in the conversations we had over the tapes, a communication that went on and on. It continued as she assisted me in Contact Improvisation classes at Antioch College in Yellow Springs. And when she and others moved to California, we continued there, under the umbrella of ReUnion, whose other members—Curt Siddall and Nita Little—and guests David Woodberry, Danny Lepkoff, and Lisa Nelson (as well as Karen Radler from an earlier California tour) also helped sculpt the performance and the teaching and the thought forms that distinguished this new improvisational form.

Truth to tell, when I think of those early years, I am apt to remember things like sliding down brown sand dunes between Arizona and Cal, coast-to-coast jaunts undertaken like trips to the corner store, understandings found in eyes, laughing at things in ESP—not so much the Contact Improvisation itself as the human contexts that made it possible to pursue. They seem conditional, personal, you-had-to-be-there-ish.

Pioneering the form gave these twenty-plus-year-olds a certain authority. We were a kind of laboratory, making our results public via performances and classes that we were invited to give. But even as it was coming together and interest was shown across the U.S. and in Canada, the personnel began to separate.

Nancy began to set up performance dates and to teach on her own. She became a sought-after teacher in North America and then in Europe. I recall a class we shared in Boulder, Colorado; she was developing new forms for the classwork! The energy of the class was kept high, without fatigue. Another instance I experienced (and enjoyed) occurred at Breitenbush Hot Springs; it was a way of critiquing the dance by committee. My group of six not only gave each other feedback but stayed up late into the night discussing the issues that Contact Improvisation raises. She was finding ways to let the form out to speak for itself, it seemed.

As when, earlier, she took on the responsibility of the *Contact Newsletter*, to provide some sort of record of what was happening to our bodies and ourselves. This evolved into *Contact Quarterly*, which continues today, edited and produced by Nancy in Massachusetts and Lisa Nelson in Vermont. It is written by dancers—at first it was contacters only, but then the magazine began to print articles on other dance forms and practices.

photo: Uldis Ohaks

Steve Paxton *[above]* and David Woodberry performing with ReUnion at the San Francisco Museum of Modern Art, 1976.

photo: Ted Pushinsky

Steve Paxton performing at Site Gallery, San Francisco, 1978.

north america

Dance magazines are terribly fragile publications. There is a certain market, usually made up of very young dance students who purchase them to see photographs of their idols in midair or high arabesque; essentially fanzines. The few intellectually oriented dance publications don't seem to last long, perhaps reflecting the difficult transition from physical and mental subservience in the dance classroom to a more mature mental comprehension of the body's physical forms.

But the *Quarterly* has had the great good luck of publishing during an era when dance and dancers have been moving conceptually and physically. Its pages provide us with the ongoing saga of Contact Improvisation, along with articles about Body-Mind Centering, Release Technique, Skinner Releasing, Action Theater, Ideokinesis, Topf Technique, yoga, tai chi, Vipassana Meditation, Feldenkrais, modern dance, capoiera, plus the adventures of dance-improvising teachers and performers in far-flung lands.

The *Quarterly*, describing itself as *A Vehicle for Moving Ideas*, has chronicled a ripple effect, from a few studios, galleries, and gymnasiums in the 1970s gently across the surface of our globe. It has given us viewpoints of this process over time. It has become the repository of the historic body of a dance form, providing us a record of birth, growth, maturity, and cross-pollination with other disciplines.

It is not predicated on the structure of art dancing, which retains from its martial heritage the pyramidal form of rigorous hierarchy. It's more on the order of the ancestral motifs of groups, picnics, potlatches, potlucks, and holidays. Temporary but renewable structures rather than grand institutional edifices.

And it is interesting to note that the Internet was born in the same year as Contact Improvisation and that they share an ethos. The *Quarterly* has become our mother node. There is a vision of communality at work, taking for granted the notion that immediate activities add byte by byte into a vast chaotic structure that, in turn, will move us together, apart; together, apart.

photo: Uldis Ohaks

Steve and Nancy performing with ReUnion at the San Francisco Museum of Modern Art, 1976.
(Clyfford Still painting in the background.)

As Contact Improvisation has enlarged geographically, it has become more inclusive socially. Ballet dancers, modern dancers, postmodern dancers, folks with disabilities, and just plain folks have ventured into the swirl of it. Apparently, a new common dance has emerged.

Nancy has not just been sitting at her desk during the past twenty-five-plus years. She has been performing all over the world, creating her own work, and been a most active teacher of Contact Improvisation.

Nancy, Lisa, and the *Quarterly* have shown devotion and endurance. I hope Nancy's long service to the field is the groundwork for further development in classes, in performance, and in print.

It is difficult for me to imagine the developments of the past quarter century without feeling gratitude for the keys Nancy has provided, the doors she has opened. She has made it possible for us to know ourselves and maintained a forum for our words and thoughts, which will give future dancers an idea of this period.

Her career thus far is unique, improbable. Take note: Her future back issues will illuminate our arts, and future backwords are, no doubt, forthcoming.

the earth

Steve Paxton
Vermont, 1999

the underscore

WHAT IT IS

The Underscore is a framework for practicing and researching dance improvisation that I've been developing since the early 1990s. It is a score that guides dancers through a series of "changing states," from solo deepening/releasing and sensitizing to gravity and support; through group circulation and interaction, Contact Improvisation (CI) engagements, opening out to full group improvisation with compositional awareness, and back to rest and reflection.

The Underscore can be seen as a vehicle for incorporating Contact Improvisation into a broader arena of improvisational practice; for developing greater ease dancing in spherical space—alone and with others; and for integrating kinesthetic and compositional concerns while improvising. The Underscore is also being used in the CI community worldwide as a way to focus and concentrate Contact jams.

A BIT OF HISTORY

I came to the Underscore—or it came to me—in 1990 after a crisis in my teaching. I had been developing and teaching Contact Improvisation for over fifteen years and had accumulated a tremendous amount of teaching material—exercises, principles, concepts, language—and had begun to feel hugely claustrophobic in having to follow my own syllabus. Where was the constant sense of discovery, the invention of materials and methods of the early years, when every class posed new challenges to the task of "passing the dance" of CI—and with them came new solutions? Classes now were too full of "must do's." Internally, I rebelled.

My rebellion came in the form of open space. I found myself prolonging open, structureless sections of class, during which I would suggest things to focus on—through language and my own movement. As we danced, I would continue to add images and concerns but never stop to form the activity into specific exercises or scores. Over the course of the session, we'd pass through silent depths and lively heights with less and less organized, structured activity and more and more "space." What was I teaching now? Nights before these workshops I was uncharacteristically sleepless. I enjoyed the classes immensely while in them, but all around them I was rather bewildered and anxious. I even considered not teaching for a while until I got clear about what I was doing.

But then one summer I noticed something. My classes were by now consisting of a changing proportion of this open "talked" space and a few specifically focused activities/exercises occurring in a seemingly random, intuitively determined order. It was 1990 and a student in my class at the two-week A Cappella Motion workshop came up and said, "You know that part of class where we get very wild and disoriented, with lots of momentum and falling and jumping?" Yes, I thought, I know what "state" you're referring to, but I didn't understand what he meant by *"that part of class."* A few days later, another student approached me to talk about "that part of class where we get deep and still, focusing on tiny sensations." Again, I recognized the state of movement and mind she was referring to, but what was this "part of class" thing? And then it dawned on me that underneath what I was experiencing as a random selection of materials was a very consistent score operating all the time, informing my choices. What was this inner, under score?

> *I remember looking at a strange and beautiful blue flower on my way to the studio one day during this week, a few days after the birth of this "under score" thought. The two have always remained linked for me. On a bush, tight rectangular clusters of pale blue/yellow buds were framed by small blue petals spraying out of the corners of the rectangle, only at the corners—an unusual brooch-like flower, something my immigrant grandmother might have worn, in pewter, on her dress or wool coat. The colors were cooling, the form surprising and delightful.*

Drawing, NSS, 1990

Fleshing out this "under-score" revelation became a compelling focus for me and the students and colleagues in my workshops over the next years. Significant phases or states of movement and mind in the improvisation were identified and named; graphic symbols were created to capture the spirit or energy of the phase without words. And thus the Underscore evolved.

The score didn't have a name for the first ten years of its existence. We used to just call it "the score." I searched for a name for many years but nothing felt right. Until finally I heard myself tell the story of its beginning and heard myself say that there was an "under score" functioning all the time. Voilà! I tried it out for a while and it stuck.

The Underscore is still in process—its components, concepts, and applications are still growing, deepening, and clarifying. I imagine that more phases will be added and others further detailed in the future. The Underscore is a form of play and research, not the law. I hope you will approach it in this spirit.

Here, now, is a short rundown of the current phases of the score. May it serve you and your dancing well:

photo: NSS

Underscore pages falling off the wall during a run of the score.

THE UNDERSCORE

( ) ARRIVING ENERGETICALLY Bringing your attention, your presence, your will, into the room. Bringing your focus into the present situation. Arriving into the present moment.

(·) ARRIVING PHYSICALLY Arriving into sensation. Focusing your attention on your physical sensations, the textures and locations of sensation throughout the body—the rise and fall of your breathing, the sensation of muscle tissue stretching, the action inside the joint, the touch of your body against the floor, your weight. Waking up to the encyclopedia of sensations in the body. I am reminded of Steve Paxton's image of "using the mind as a lens into the body." Magnifying sensation with attention.

Arriving physically is arriving into "body time"—where there's enough time to register your sensations and absorb their information and "nutritional value" into your system (rather than just accomplishing a physical task). Becoming present in your body.

POW-WOW Taking time to check in with the others who will be practicing the score: to introduce ourselves, set time parameters, mention any physical conditions we want others to be aware of and any other necessary practical information. It's also a time to "plant seeds" into our practice for the day—specific ideas and curiosities that anyone in the group is bringing into the Underscore that day.

It is not always necessary to do this, but we usually do.

PREAMBULATION Circulating through the dance space by walking, running, or other simple variations. Time to see the room and the environment outside the room, to see each other, and to feel your own movement through space. Arriving into your movement, the space, and the community of people you're practicing with.

This is especially useful after a *pow-wow;* but even if there hasn't been a meeting, it's a nice way to begin the next progression of states.

SKINESPHERE A made-up term, *skinesphere* refers to the movement arena inside the boundary of your skin—that is, the sensation of movement and change inside your body. Turning on, and becoming aware of, the movement inside the body mass—all the wriggling, weight pouring, shifting, lengthening, contracting, falling, torquing, flowing, compressing, elating, sequencing, settling, exploding/imploding movement activity that happens inside your body but that doesn't move you through space very much. There are two main aspects of *skinesphere* that I've identified so far:

BONDING WITH THE EARTH Releasing your weight to the ground. Establishing a feelable sensation of the mass/weight of your body and its connection with and support from the mass of the earth.

One way: Surrendering your weight to the floor, lying down, releasing muscle tone/tension, letting go, letting down. Feeling the sensation of falling through the body and the complementary sensation of support coming up from the mass of the earth—the support rising up from the ground in equal measure to meet your release, radiating support throughout your mass, your skeleton, etc. Resting in this sensation of release, falling, and support.

This sensation of release and support can be felt in many positions, including standing upright, feeling the "small dance of standing" (Steve Paxton), when the body relaxes excess muscle tension to find balanced skeletal support and to experience the small adjustments that the body makes reflexively to remain balanced on two legs. This is the "small dance," a primary reference in the training for Contact Improvisation.

MOBILIZING/AGITATING THE MASS Stimulating the *skinesphere* in another way. Gently shaking and loosening the mass, actively engaging in generating your own movement (rather than a passive release to gravity). Mobilizing different mass areas—thigh, pelvis, rib cage, head—soothing and stimulating the body through motion, energizing and separating the "particles of mass" for greater articulation and readiness later on.

I sometimes offer the "shakedown" for this—moving sequentially through the body with this mobilizing/shaking action—but it can be done in other ways.

Mobilizing can come before, after, or alternate with *bonding with the earth.*

KINESPHERE Extending your movement, energy, attention, awareness, curiosity, desire into the space around the body. Moving out into the environment from *skinesphere* into the space around the body by increasing tone, stretching, reaching, condensing, pushing.

The *kinesphere*, coined by Rudolf Laban, is the sphere or bubble of space around the body through which one can reach and move one's limbs without changing the placement of one's center. In the Underscore, *kinesphere* is divided into "low" and "high." I experience a marked difference between these zones when I'm warming up toward full mobility through spherical space.

LOW KINESPHERE Opening up movement pathways through your *kinesphere* when your center is either on or close to the floor—rolling, crawling, scooting, sliding, and other forms of locomotion through the low space, from the floor up to about two or three feet above the floor.

The height of your *low kinesphere* would roughly be the distance between your sitz bones and the top of your head or outstretched arms or legs. In terms of warming up, this zone would include all manner of movement that prepares you to fall and recover and safely pass through the space from the floor up to about waist height. I sometimes focus on "the last six inches" when teaching and use that focus to develop strategies for safe landings, slides, rolls, and rebounds into and off of the floor. All the many rolling patterns—somersaults, aikido rolls, crescent and spiral rolls—and all the developmental movement patterns (crawling, etc.) greatly support this mobility through the *low kinesphere*.

HIGH KINESPHERE Extending your movement and energy/attention through mid-heights to standing level and even off your feet. Working toward mobility in all directions through the sphere, whether initiating from head, toe, center; from an internal desire to move outward or an attraction to something in the space that draws you out; or from any other motivation for moving. Taking advantage of the *low kinesphere* activity that came before, as now the techniques for rolling and falling and moving are extended through greater distances and heights. Integrating *high* with *low kinesphere*, working to transition comfortably between them.

EXPANDING/TRAVELING KINESPHERE

Extending your attention and mobility through more space, either by *expanding the size* of your sphere of movement and awareness, or by *traveling* that sphere through the space.

Expanding and *traveling* are distinct but can overlap. For instance, you might be moving within a small sphere close to the body and might enjoy rolling or traveling within that cocoon of space through the rest of the room. Or, conversely, you might enlarge your perception of and exchange with the space to include the whole room but continue to move in one area and not travel much. Or you can expand *and* travel. This expansion (or contraction) refers to both the range of your reception and your transmission of energy and activity—your intake and output, perception and action.

OVERLAPPING KINESPHERES

In a roomful of people warming up in this manner, the *kinespheres* of the dancers—the space through which their energy, movement, and attention are circulating—will overlap one another. This sensation of moving past and through someone's "space" (and of being passed) "stirs the pot," generates energy, and primes the dancers for further connections.

In *overlapping kinespheres*, you're moving through the landscape of different movement qualities and characteristics without interpreting the information yet; taking the ride like a hawk over a summer hillside.

photo: Raisa Kyllikki Karjalainen

In the Underscore, Helsinki, Finland, 2007. *[Left to right]* Mirva Mäkinen, Ronja Verkasalo, Ulla Mäkinen, [*hidden*: Iiris Raipala, Sini Haapalinna], Ville Johansson, NSS.

GRAZING

Warming up to interaction with others and the environment through a series of short *connections*—perceptual *connections* (e.g., you see a *coincidence*) and physical *connections* (your path of movement comes together with another mover's in a *confluence* and a *touch*). Noticing *connections* that you are a part of and those that occur between others. Allowing your solo dance to pass into, through, and between any of these *connections*, in any order. This is *grazing*.

X CONNECTIONS *(in no particular order):*

TOUCH

Allowing physical contact between your body and another body or object. All manner of incidental, accidental, and intentional touches—glancing, sliding, bumping, light, weighted, peripheral, central, indirect, direct, unexpected, intentional. Touch can also be experienced as a kind of measure of space and body. How long is your arm? How far is that body?

ATTRACTION

Sensing a pull *toward* something or someone—another dancer's movement quality, presence, body mass; the music; a patch of sunlight on the floor. Feeling a magnetic pull to touch, move with, move toward.

REPULSION

Sensing your energy moving *away* from something or someone—a movement, object, sound, activity, body. Not a personal, social judgment but a momentary impulse to go in a different direction—*away from*. This could change in an instant.

One can choose to go with or resist any impulse.

COINCIDENCE

Same thing, same time. Having fun noticing different kinds of coincidences occurring throughout the dancing environment:

In movement: Two people falling at the exact same moment in different parts of the room; three dancers running at the same speed; several people standing still at the same time, or moving with the same quality.

In sound: You exhale a deep breath and hear someone else across the room doing the same thing at the same moment; as your body meets the floor in a fall, the music stops.

In color: You notice two people dancing together both wearing red and black; everyone in your trio is wearing a shade of turquoise.

Atemporal coincidences: Similar things happening at *different* times. An explosive solo occurs in one corner of the room and much later in the session there's another very similar solo taking place in the same spot.

INTERSECTION

Crossing paths—in front, behind, close, far.

CONFLUENCE Two paths flowing into one. Can be a literal coming into physical contact—a confluence of mass—or just a synchronizing of movement pathways, qualities, timing, or ideas.

DIVERGENCE A common path splitting into two or more paths.

CONTRAST Acknowledging difference. Noticing more extreme differences of speed, quality, spatial level, "state," direction. Being aware of contrast in any aspect of one's movement, activity, presence, as well as in the environment.

For instance, you're deep in a *skinespheric* release of your weight and someone else is on fire, running around the room dancing big and wild in their *expanded, traveling kinesphere.* There is no pressure to change. Acknowledge *contrast.*

INFLUENCE Noticing *influence* of one thing on another—someone runs through the room and moments later the energy level of the group goes up; there is music with a strong beat and suddenly half the group takes on the rhythm; you realize you've picked up the quality of someone moving past you. Changes of speed, quality, rhythm, intensity, mood, direction—these influences can be noticed after or while they're occurring, can be intentionally chosen or inhibited, can occur between you and others or be observed in others.

EMPATHY/RESONANCE This is different from *attraction* in that you might feel a sympathetic *resonance* with someone or something but not necessarily a desire to come closer or join him/her/it.

COLLISION Coming into direct and forceful physical contact with someone or something. *Collisions* can be soft, intentional or not, generally accompanied by a rebound off the other body. Perhaps there could also be energetic (nonphysical) collisions? Collisions of qualities or ideas?

TANGENT A single moment of two paths or worlds coming into (and then out of) contact.

MORE: It is fun to make up new ones as we go along. Noticing what occurs.

ENGAGEMENT After a while of *grazing* through short *touches* and other *connections*, one allows oneself to stay or be drawn further into a touch connection and to fully "engage." You're no longer on your way somewhere, tasting short exchanges along the way. You're in until it's over. This is *engagement.* We often use the first long *engagement* of the score as an opportunity to focus on the development of a Contact Improvisation dance—a CI warm-up dance.

Eventually in the score, an *engagement* can be any sort of *connection* that you decide to develop—whether it's a Contact Improvisation or a touch connection, or a nontouch connection based on timing, image, shape, imagination, quality, rhythm, or sound—with one or more people or as a soloist.

DEVELOPMENT As soon as one *engages,* the dance naturally *develops*—deepens, unfolds, one thing leading to the next. This is true whether it's a Contact Improvisation duet, a trio, or any number of people involved in another improvised event in the space. Once there is *engagement*, things immediately start to develop.

RESOLUTION/END/DISENGAGEMENT Ending the *engagement* can be sensed or chosen in many ways. It is an opportunity to be aware of how things *end*—noticing what happens and/or intentionally exercising different options. It can *resolve* mutually, be interrupted, be ended by one person. It can finish crisply, gradually; drift apart with a lingering sense of connection; or complete itself unexpectedly and be over. Did it seem to resolve or just cut off? Was there a series of endings?

After ending, there is a *disengagement,* a physical and energetic departure from the form that has just ended. Again, notice how it happens, what one's own tendencies are; play with the possibilities and stay with it.

RECIRCULATION THRU SCORE Now, after the end of your first *engagement,* you're free to move anywhere in the score—into *skinesphere,* or *traveling kinesphere,* or *grazing,* or another *engagement.* Many of the phases can overlap as well—for example, you might be in a *solo engagement* and notice a *coincidence* in the room, or you're in *skinesphere* and notice you're being "grazed on" by another dancer. You are now in the *open score.*

OPEN SCORE
– WITH OBSERVING & REENTERING

Now we are jamming—physically, energetically, compositionally, experientially. *Connections* can be any length, can be Contact Improvisations or other sorts of improvised movement encounters based on timing, space, image, form, state, architecture, musicality. This can include solo or group *engagements*. Forms arise, develop, end, transition, and continue in a constant flux of life and form through myriad dynamics and levels of agreement and individuation in the space.

The *open score* lasts as long as time allows.

Observing and reentering the *open score:* At some point during the *open score*, dancers can individually step out of the frame of activity and **observe,** and several minutes later **reenter,** finding their way back into the improvisation. This is an important function of the score and is done with the intention of supporting, studying, and enjoying. There are many possible filters for looking at the activity. Some possible filters/lenses for observing:

- **as phenomena**—noticing forms organizing from apparent chaos, cohering, developing, changing, ending, coming apart, dissolving, transitioning
- **through the lens of the Underscore**—noticing how an *engagement* resolves and ends; catching the moment that a *grazing connection* turns into an *engagement;* witnessing someone transition from *skinesphere* to *kinesphere;* enjoying a *coincidence*
- **as a composition**—seeing relationships between formal elements—shapes, colors, movement qualities, states; framing small areas of the space in one's awareness to limit the canvas, or zooming out to be aware of the big picture
- **as physical dancing**—getting technical and kinesthetic transmissions and impressions
- **as a** big, open movement, Contact and improvisation **jam**
- **as a "village,"** with many interdependent coexisting activities (the "village" image for improvised movement in a group environment came from Suprapto Suryodarmo)
- **Any way YOU SEE IT**

I often recommend that participants *not* choose the moment right after *resolution/end/disengagement* to go out to watch but instead find another moment to step out. The time right after an *engagement* ends is a delicate moment in an improvisation, and it is interesting to support the continuity there—to see what arises in that transition rather than cutting it off to go out and watch or drink water.

FINAL RESOLUTION OF THE ROOM

At some point, it is announced—"Five minutes to *final resolution*"—or understood by previous agreement that we have only a few minutes left for dancing. This means that it is time to begin one's last chapter and, within the next minutes, to arrive at an end to one's current activity, bringing to *resolution* the development of one's own movement/dance throughout the entire length of the score. This resolution can occur as stillness or as a sustaining of the current movement image—that is, not allowing it to develop further. In this way, each individual (and the group) arrives at a common stable end point and holds it until everyone has arrived at a resolution. Sometimes "end" or "resolution" is called; more often, we sense it as a group. Everyone stays within this *final resolution* for several moments—feeling it, zooming in and out in space and time, and remaining until satisfied and complete.

DISENGAGEMENT FROM THE WHOLE PATTERN

After the *final resolution* has occurred, each individual takes him- or herself out of the final arrangement on his or her own timing. This is not a group break. Rather, each person *disengages from the whole pattern* individually and goes directly into a period of *reflection/harvest*.

REFLECTION/HARVEST

Taking time on one's own to rest, warm down, review, and reflect on one's experience during the score. We move directly from the *final resolution* into *reflection* without socializing and other interaction.

This is time to reflect on your experience through writing, moving, drawing, and thinking—gleaning direct observations that can be shared with others. How did the score function for you this time? What is one specific thing that happened? What did you perceive, feel, learn? These are your gleanings, your field notes; not full summaries or interpretations. They might just be fragments.

I love the way the room feels during this phase—a spacious, calm atmosphere where we can be alone together, reflecting on our experiences dancing and improvising in the score.

SHARING/THANKSGIVING

This is a time to come together (often in a circle or group) to offer reflections, some "fruits" of the harvest. Usually short remarks with little or no cross-talk discussion. No need for big "summings" up, just a small bit of true observation from one's experience is plenty. (You can also "pass" if you don't have anything to share or don't feel like talking.) The expressions of intelligence and awareness and the variety of experiences in this *sharing* are remarkable, informative, and amusing. The observations act as a way of composting or fertilizing our practice, informing the path for the next time around. Sometimes it's nice to have some fruit or other easy snack to share during this phase, especially if the score has been going for three hours by this point.

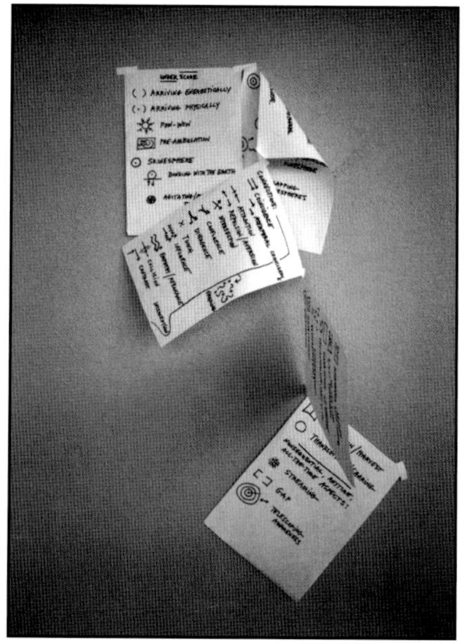

photo: NSS

Underscore pages falling.

Nonsequential Anytime All-the-Time Aspects

Some principles and phenomena to consider, use, and notice throughout your practice of the Underscore.

Streaming *Streaming* is a sense of the ongoing flow of your energy and life force, continuous as long as you are alive. Whether you're happy or sad, engaged or bored, alone or with others, clear or unclear about what you're doing, underneath it all, you're *streaming*. Awareness of this, and connection with it, can become useful at various points along the way. For me, a visual equivalent is the streaming particles of light on the screen before a film starts, the leader at the start of the reel—an ongoing field of little dots of light moving toward you, not yet focused into a particular image.

Breathing seems to be connected with *streaming*. The constriction of one can likewise affect the other. This is another reason to keep your breathing comfortable and flowing. Reminding yourself to breathe or to consider *streaming* can be especially helpful if you're feeling dull, lost, panicked, or stuck. It can help you "suspend disbelief" and judgment and begin noticing what is happening in your inner and outer environment, relax, and feel what attracts you.

[ ] Gap *Gaps* are moments in the improvisation where you experience a temporary absence of reference, a feeling of being between forms and not sure what's happening or what to do. This can even occur inside known forms (inside a Contact Improvisation duet, for instance). These moments of *gap* can last fractions of a second or longer and can be responded to in many ways. You might choose to do something familiar and fill the gap in that way. Or you might just breathe, *stream*, and notice points of reference beginning to occur, eventually organizing into a discernible form. Hang out in the gap and see what happens. On some days, for some people, *gaps* are difficult and undesirable; on other days, they are exciting, funny, fascinating encounters with the unknown.

Study how you feel, what you perceive, what you do in these moments, and notice others' ways too. Being relaxed and alert, with a sense of concentration and humor, is generally a useful stance.

Telescoping Awareness Adjusting the scale and focus of one's awareness at any time—a zoom lens. Choosing to zoom in on a tiny sensation inside the body, or telescoping out to be aware of one's whole body at once, or widening the view to encompass your body and the space around it, or going further out to include the whole room in your view.

This *telescoping* out and in allows one to get information at various levels and also to develop the ability to concentrate on different levels of information at different moments. For instance, if you become aware that you've been focusing internally for a while, it could be interesting to telescope out to check where you are in the room and what else is going on around you, near and far, without losing your connection to the physical sensations you are engaged with. One can then play between views.

Telescoping awareness is a tool that you can use any time—to get different compositional views, to relieve claustrophobia or overstimulation by enlarging or limiting your field of awareness, and to work with several dimensions/layers concurrently.

Idiot Button Press it whenever things have gotten too complex. It simplifies and reduces everything to the basics—presence, breath, sensation...and now what? The *idiot button* is a handy alternative to completely shutting down.

Listening Keeping your ears and other senses open. Noticing the sound and its connection and coexistence with what you're doing and what's happening in the room.

THE END

Ending the *sharing/thanksgiving* time and closing the Underscore can be done formally or informally—with silence, a bell, sharing of food, a simple thanks and good-bye.

The post-score resolution/disengagement behavior can also be fun to note as we check clocks; debrief further with partners; socialize; take care of body, clothes, other business; wander around a bit dazed; and eventually leave the room, carrying on with our lives.

photo: NSS

Underscore pages above the heater.

PRACTICE NOTES

All "in" all the time. From the moment you enter the room until we finish the *sharing*, you're in the score no matter what you do. You're never "out." Everything is part of the composition of the score until we close—even going to the toilet *(expanding/traveling kinesphere!)*.

Contact experience necessary? My assumption has been that people practicing the Underscore would already have some experience with Contact Improvisation. The CI form itself is simple in principle but demanding in practice and, in my opinion, is best served when given the time to be learned purely as its own dance form and not mixed with too many other concerns. So, I generally propose the Underscore as a practice for people already experienced in the form of CI and probably other improvisational dance forms as well. It is not intended as an introduction to Contact but as a framework in which to apply it.

Does the Underscore make sense on its own? I usually present the Underscore in the context of workshops where many layers of physical, perceptual, and conceptual reference and vocabulary are established in our sessions and applied to phases of the score. Given only the structure of the score with no other information, I am not sure how much sense it makes. However, for most contacters and many contemporary dance improvisers, the phases of the Underscore are self-evident, and most dancers already have plenty of their own references to bring to it.

What materials can be included? Especially in the *open score*, there is the question of how broad the palette of usable materials should be for the Underscore. What about bringing in text? Making sound? Theater? Social exchange? Ballet vocabulary, Authentic Movement, modern dance, yoga, capoeira? Painting? Photography?

For my interests, and for the coherence of the practice, I think it is useful to focus the Underscore on movement improvisation and not venture too far into text and theatricality. If there is a musician improvising with the score, I prefer to let him or her make the music. If the dancers are moved to make sound, I encourage them to be especially mindful of their collaboration with the musician.

But there are no absolute rules (yet?). Though the focus is definitely on movement (with the welcome inclusion of Contact Improvisation), each practicing group will determine what materials they are interested in including while staying true to the intention of the Underscore as they understand it. There are of course limits, but we have to reach them to discover them. The form is still too young to know what they all are and why. And who sets the limits? Me? Or do the people who are currently in the room practicing the score set the limits? Probably, and ideally, it will be a combination of both.

Leadership. Introducing a new group or individuals to the Underscore requires some preparation—a talk through the phases before the practice, or some guidance or suggestion during the session, or a combination of both. It makes a difference to feel that all the players have the elements of the score in mind, consciously functioning within their improvisation. At least some of the time. Ultimately, with a group of people who have all practiced the Underscore before, it is not necessary for anyone to direct or lead the practice, only perhaps to keep the time.

Time and timing. The Underscore usually runs between two and four hours from start to finish but can be reduced or expanded to any length of time. It is good to establish the overall time frame at the beginning of the practice if not before.

The timing of changes from one phase to another within the score can initially be guided by a teacher or score leader but is eventually open. Once open, the evolution of states proceed according to your personal timing, based on your physical condition, desire, and intention for that run. Timings for each phase can vary greatly from one run to the next; phases might overlap, go forward and back, occur in a slightly different order, or be skipped altogether. Differences in timings between individual players make for new circumstances/compositions to work with during the improvisation.

Music or no music? For most of my years of practicing Contact and the early years of the Underscore, I usually preferred working without music, keeping the timings, rhythms, moods, and states of the dancing purely in the hands of the dancers. In the late 1990s, I was fortunate enough to come into contact with a most intelligent and sensitive improvising composer, Mike Vargas, with whom I've been working ever since. We are finding ways to increase the listening of the dancers while factoring into the music-making a permeability and proportion of silence that seems to allow for the best of both worlds—independence, awareness, and a variety of possible relationships. When there's music, it's important that the dancers continue to work with the timing of the body, imagination, and physical forces while relating to the live music with integrity, variety, awareness, and choice. Initially, this might mean actively inhibiting habitual responses to the music. Mike and I have been finding it useful to suggest that all the possible *connections* listed in the Underscore (for example, *attraction, coincidence, contrast,* and *influence*) can easily apply to the relationship between the music and the dance, between what we hear and how we move.

photo: Barbara Stahlberger

Mike Vargas playing for a jam at the Freiburg Contact Festival, Freiburg, Germany, August 2005.

Talking or no talking? During the Underscore, I ask people not to talk so that all the energy can be focused on dancing and supporting the dancing through watching.

Intentions. There seem to be as many reasons why people like to practice the Underscore as there are reasons to dance. One's intention—to study, play, make art, work out, relax, dance, research, meditate, and more—at any moment is a strong factor affecting the choices he or she makes within the improvisation.

Is the Underscore descriptive or prescriptive? Does it simply describe what tends to happen or is it suggesting what to do? Probably a little of both.

Balancing perceiving and action. Balancing your noticing/perceiving and your action is an important part of the discipline of improvisation. Thinking too much or being hyperaware may cut off a sense of spontaneity and flow and instinct, whereas being impulsive or lost in sensation can reduce awareness and thus limit the levels of play that you can track and participate in.

Can't do it wrong. As long as your intention is to do the Underscore (and you haven't inadvertently mistaken this for a tango class or nightclub), you can relax and assume that your actions and interpretations won't be "wrong." During the *harvest*, it can be interesting to reflect on actions that were experienced by you or others as being out of the frame of this practice and why. Discernment of all kinds is constantly functioning, but it's an unnecessary waste of energy to worry if you're doing it right while it's going on. Assume that you are.

Often I'll try to talk through the phases of the score with the group on the day before our first practice of the Underscore. This gives everyone a chance to let go of the words and ideas, digest them in their sleep, and come to the dancing fresh, without so many thoughts and ideas in the forefront of their attention. Time for the concepts to drop to the background and let the present sensations and feelings of the dancing be in "front."

And now, on to the dancing!

Nancy Stark Smith
2008

Enormous thanks to the many students and colleagues who have contributed to the research, articulation, and practice of the Underscore over the years. Your enthusiastic engagement with the work has been an inspiration and has provided many valuable insights and materials to the Underscore at each phase of its development.

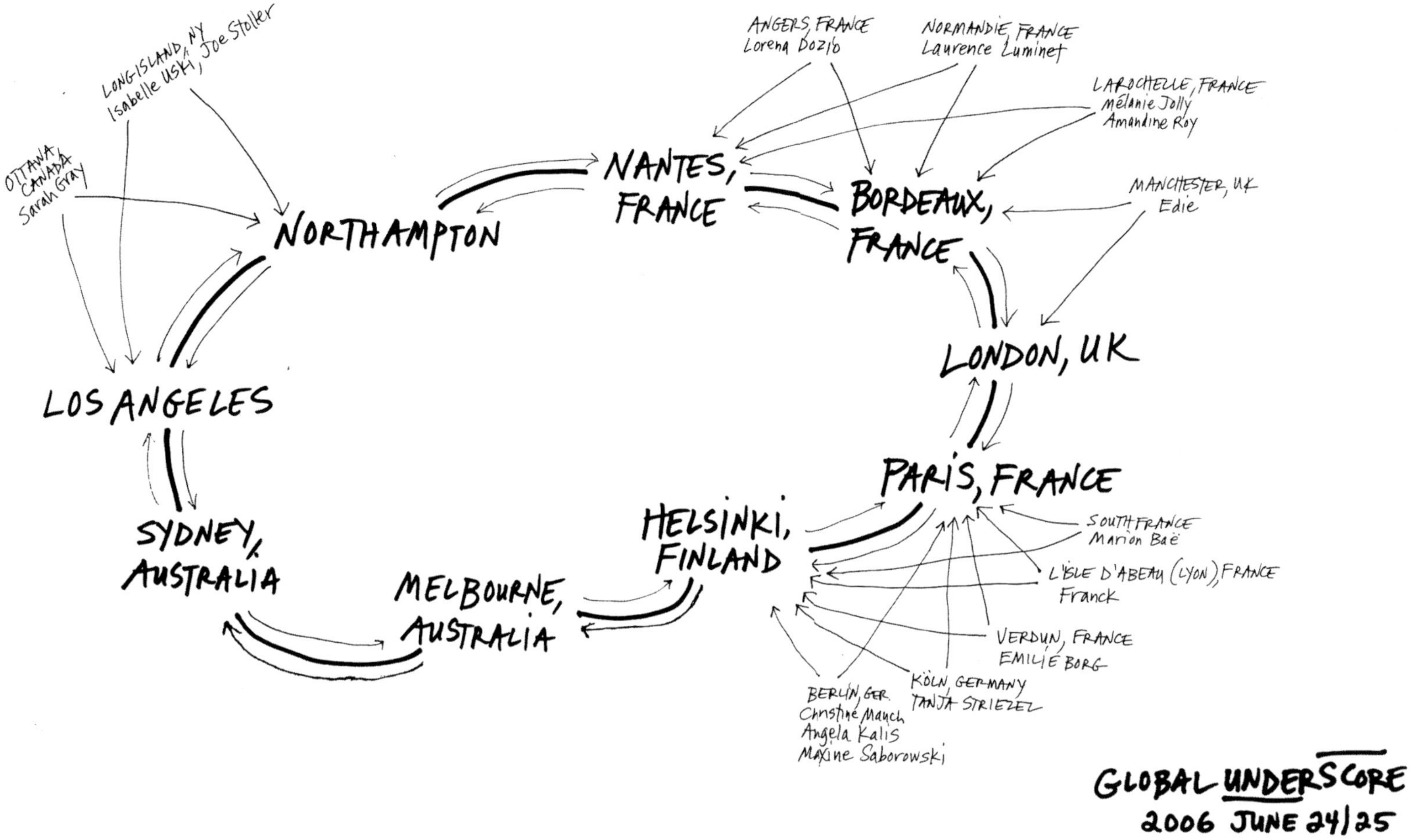

The Global Underscore. The Underscore continues to spread as people bring it back to their jams and dance communities around the world. In 2000, Claire Filmon and Laura Porter Blackburn, in Paris, organized a Global Underscore on the June solstice—a simultaneous four-hour run of the score, with many participating sites around the globe (some dancing in the middle of the night). During an opening and closing "small dance," each group faces the next around the orb—facing east at the beginning and facing west at the end. Individual "satellites," dancers not part of a bigger group practice that day, can link in too. The Global Underscore Solstice became an annual event organized by Claire and the Paris Underscore group. This was the map for 2006. Green arrows indicated facings for the opening stand, red arrows for the closing stand.

photo: Catherine Magill

The "small dance" in Sydney, Australia, during Global Underscore 2006, on the cover of *Proximity* magazine, an Australian Contact and improvisation journal; Vol. 9:2, August 2006.

epi-chrono-logue

photo: Bruce Newhouse

David Koteen on a sculpture by Paul Pappas in Eugene, OR, 1993.

MARCH 1991
Pre-Conception, this book,
with an almost falling
accidental crimson rose...
and revelation
"BROKEN HEART MEANS OPEN HEART"
which led directly to
Raku,
Nancy's then new, and yet ongoing, solo.
At Breitenbush annual CI Jam
seeking reflection, she showed me
Raku

MARCH 24, 1994

Dear David,
Sy asked me to thank you for your idea to interview Nancy Stark Smith for The Sun. *Your enthusiasm for her is convincing; we'd like to see the interview.*

Pamela Penick
Assistant Editor

From 1985 to 1990, prior to *Raku* and the falling rose incident, I had more observed Nancy from afar: teaching, laughing, singing, skipping—being best friends with her body—running backwards (eyes closed, standing by river in sun with red beret), headstand with braid swishing like panther's tail. Seamlessly fearless. We shared an occasional dance, lunch, happenstance, flash dialogue, random meeting. In Nancy I found a sophisticated sororal ally. An amphibious monkey creature, who, like me, luxuriated in movement, romance, service, and freedom.

My Self had become rededicated to the principle of self-liberation through assistance to others on their respective paths...and here she was, Nancy, embracing her own karma, being her own gravity.

We shared a craving for precise language, art/icu/lation. Giving things their proper names. I suggested an interview, or intra-view, or VIEWS: our first working title.

I had been published on and off by *The Sun* magazine and wrote editor Sy Safransky, January 1994, about interviewing NSS on CI for *The Sun*.

Because *Raku* was/is
so delicate and tranquil, my unique
suggestion was to perform in front of white cloth
or sheet. Nancy invited me to come out from
the audience (at Eugene's WOW Hall post-
Breitenbush annual performance) & place afore-noted
white sheet, appropriately, on the dance floor.
We agreed to meet where she was staying, at Steve
Christiansen's (videographer of early CI)
house, pre-performance—

SEPTEMBER 8, 1994

*NANCY ... hi, ... here's ze track I lit on.
Started with the ole telephone pretend
conversation score, soon segueing into
normalish interview with you about mutually
attractive ideas/issues: CI and intimacy and
politics and transformation and healing through
touch and playfulness, being precise and abstract
as is Aquarianistically possible. I decided to
number by D's to facilitate moving them around.*
Lotsaffection David

*D-1: Nancy ... hi ... Do you know who this is,
calling from green and lush western Oregon?*

Being enamored with Nancy was easy, teaching with laughter, teeming with life. INTERVIEW I. I had set my little tape recorder next to a speaker phone downstairs while I chatted with Nancy on upstairs phone. The result was fifty-five pages transcribed by a 65-year-old born-again Christian typist on "Contract [Im]Problemization." We've used nothing from this interview—except its intrinsic fertility.

OCTOBER 10, 1994

Yo, Nancy ... "the interview" is too vague. Hence, the 2nd set of questions I'm sending are of more mundane nature. For The Sun *article with these new questions and original 14, introductions, and some photos, perhaps lengthy captions, and selected excerpts from first interview, then ... voila!*
Cider and fires to ya ... David

Enroute to Steve Christiansen's
I bought bright red rose from blind woman
on 13th Street...and placed it stem and
all, behind my left ear. I
showed Nancy my selection of "white sheets"
...& shortly thereafter found myself
sitting at WOW Hall, waiting my debut
as "white sheet" spreader...

Clearly, there was too much material already for a mere article... Hey, Nancy, how's about a full-fledged book...?

I typed up three series of questions, following my own wishes and intuitions and whims, leaving different-sized-spaces for Nancy to respond in.

MAY 13, 1997

Dearest Nancy ... things seem today to be especially glorious greens and singing to my heart. To start, 1 gift: mountain lion came off the hill, some golden, primitive apparition, hit pavement (Fox Hollow Road) this side of double yellow line & then passed my windshield over guardrail & down hill, out of sight—140 lbs., 5 ft. long, 36 inches at ears. Courage to you. It's comin in bounds & leaps.

Whatever you send I'll employ to create our next take proto-type book entity by CI25. May 19, 20, is soon enuf.
Love is where you find it
" " " " get "
David

AUGUST 29, 1997

Hello to you ... several meetings later with Joel Southern [our Eugene graphics man] integrating Simone's notes, our past x-changes, personal prejudices, letting go of last working title, and ... and ... and if we can determine the page layout afore you go to Far East, Joel will add to our already 70 megabyte file ... and I'll be further inspired to create more & more & more ... love ... David

NOVEMBER 18, 1997

Nancy … Sending some wild orchid thoughts
To balance cultural mayhem & roles
People lay on you … not for your
Benefit … Peace, Sister …

Caught by Surprise *does seem to fit.*
Beside "comet comments" [these would be
somehow intimate associates of NSS relating
personal vivid recollections—arriving, as it were, from
"outer space"] … why so many variables?

Though still weak-in-head (one month since
temporal area tumor removal) looking towards
immersion in our project … soon.
I am well overwhelmed by Healing support
available … if I'm able to ask?
Be Gentle with Your
Precious Self
David

From off-green WOW Hall dressing
room I am easily visible to Nancy.
Like Lauren Bacall, nonchalantly
I saunter out
& do my "white sheet spreader" thing…leaving
one corner dog-eared.
& then like Harpo Marx
feigning to leave stage I return,
un-dogear fourth corner of white
sheet, allowing beauteous
blind woman's crimson rose
accidentally (almost) to fall…
The audience quieted quickly.
Nancy gasped.
Raku began.

December 1997. We met in New York City and drove to Virginia retreat Workspace for Choreographers chez Sally Nash…singing Beatles' songs and Broadway show tunes. One week in hibernal deciduous forest dancin', cookin', writin', Tarot Cards, chilly walks, reassessin' each other and "the book project." Final day we picked yarrow stalks and inquired of *I-Ching* oracle: Perseverance Furthers…

Caught by Surprise

was now 8 1/2" x 17" with pasted-on images from NSS's family, friends, lovers, dance partners… She drove me to Washington and I flew home.

DECEMBER 30, 1998

Dear Nancy and David,
Thanks for writing—I'm glad to know
how the book is coming along
(although immediately have my
own opinion: what? smaller format?
why? the big format is ESSENTIAL!). What
do I know? Every project goes through
its own evolution. However, from some
recent experience with people here who
work through feedback—don't get detoured
by everyone who wants to tell you how to do
it. What do they know?
Love, Sally [Nash]

photo: Terra Montgomery

David in *Sphenoid*, Eugene, OR, 1995.

In '98 and '99 I come to Northampton to work with Nancy, utilizing her home and *Contact Quarterly* office. One week per visit. Further circumscribing/redesigning/redefining. Would Steve Paxton be willing to write a Backwords for our book? …and this constant eerie, slightly irritating sound, like the biting wind of Winter: "Who are you—Nancy and David—in this process?"

MARCH 26, 1999

Lila is cool—we chatted & chased
ideas about book easily with laughter: what
do we want her to do?

Question for Steve's Backwords: "As significant fulcrum
of post-modern dance, would you de-dress Contact
Improvisation historically, and inside there,
Imagine Nancy Stark Smith?"

I planted 4 apple trees in swampy jardin
aujourd'hui. My heart is brimful & sloshing.
Vultures return from South, scanning
Standing broken grasses for lunch ...

Daffodils & narcissi (for whom
Echoes die) ... and evening bring
ruts and puddles, rants and
Rhymes of insipid frogs ... David

photo: NSS

David waiting for the train in Springfield, MA, after the July 2002 book retreat in Northampton, MA.

Nancy is teaching at SFADI [Seattle Festival of Alternative Dance and Improvisation] in Seattle this summer of 2000. Joan Hanna has graciously offered us use of her space on Vashon Island prior to the festival. Dancer and graphic artist Lila Hurwitz, who is designing *Contact Quarterly,* joins us for two days. Lila has mocked up the latest version of *Caught by Surprise,* streaming out the Q & A along lefthand margin and placing photos appropriately. Aaaah! this is progress.

Nan and I continue through the week, now envisioning the book as having 108 8 1/2" x 14" pages, including title page, table of contents, dedications, copyright page, and legend prior to the body of the text. The inside back cover will be a birthday poem incantation written by Christina Svane for Nancy. The last morning on Vashon we await the ferry, sitting in a small cafe. Nancy the editor/publisher projects a budget for the creation of the book.

July 2002. Over the next eighteen months our communication—emails, postcards, and occasional telephone check-ins—is sparse. What to do next? Prior to our July 2002 retreat in Northampton, Nancy has shown the book to friend and colleague Simone Forti; as well, she has invited editorial feedback from David Gere. Their comments are copious, indicating just how far we still have to go.

I depart overwhelmed, somewhat frustrated, and perplexed?!

On my return flight to Oregon, I have a minor epiphany, emerging out of one favorite CI maxim (see Q & A): *If at first you don't succeed, try less.*

August 2002. I temporarily sign off, letting NSS do what she needs to do to reconcile finishing. She lets go of Underscore and "life stories" texts for this book, shifting the center of *Caught* back to its rightful place twixt DK and NSS and CI.

December 2002 and May 2003. Nancy does solo book retreats. In February with four other Aquarians I've just completed a twelve-piece dance performance entitled *Patience, Compassion and Gratitude*. We're having a little celebration at my forested home just south of Eugene. It's drizzling and I decide to light a bonfire by pouring some gasoline on it. And end up igniting my shoulder-length hair, scorching my forehead and right arm. Oops! At the invite of chère amie Mollie, I move to Marseille for several months. During Nancy's solo retreat in May we confer several times by phone. Mollie asks: How's it going?

December 2003. In our separation, the project is well-served and has advanced under Nancy's caring, creative vision. We meet in Mamaroneck, NY—home of N's sister, Susan—and once again drive to Workspace for Choreographers in Virginia. Our relationship to one another and to *Caught* has been revitalized.

It's cold and pristine in Rappahannock County. The wind gusts through the leafless trees; dead branches crack and fall, disturbing last night's blanket of snow. The air is clear and crisp. Inside there is fire.

2004 was the year of redoubting.
I felt that Nancy and I were in some sort of mirrored labyrinth—fleeting glances, oblique dances—beauty in every reflection... But what about completing the project? The Promised Land. Celebrate...and move to the next phase of our relationship. You can only be caught by surprise for so long. What can I say—eleven years later? She made me do it.

In November, early December, Nancy, Mike Vargas, and Peter Bingham were to perform their trio, *Baseline*, in Vancouver (B.C.), Seattle, and Eugene, followed by a week of focused book furthering...and it turned out superfine!

1. Watching Nancy perform, I rediscovered my natural faith. I remembered not to divide my Self. Let doubt have a time-out. I vividly see (saw again) that our entire ongoing process together has been an intertwining time-lapse bloom. Karmic hoedown. Irregularly faceted emerald.

2. December 12 we have dinner with my dear friend Helen Bright Crosswell—astrologiste par excellance—who said to us in her well-manicured Georgian drawl, "Looks like a Jupiter cycle to me; yup, twelve-year gestation; 2006 will be perfect for healthy delivery." Bright has two young children and often speaks in baby similes.

3. By now we had accumulated roughly 600 megabytes of graphics and text, which required cleanup and rendering for our somewhat unusual 8 1/2" x 14" top-opening book. Enter Dave Snider—yeah! "El Dave" had assisted me in beaucoup art projects over the years. He grabbed Nancy's fancy in his first ten minutes of computer graphic wizardry. We agreed that Dave and I would continue to create the next version of *Caught* by May 1, 2005, when we three would convene in Northampton.

4. Just before Nancy and Mike were flying East, Nancy and I went to Eugene's Kinko's to print out hard copies of this week's work. We were feeling the intimated joy of completion. Maybe later was coming sooner? Why not 2006? We slipped our disk in to print out our copies—and lo and behold! There was something left in the copy machine. This was it:

unknown origin
The Kinko's angel.

July 13, 2006. Oops! Even with the Kinko angel on our team, another year slips by. We miss our Jupiter cycle deadline, plunge into the thirteenth year. July 8, I join my family in upstate NY for my mother's memorial. Afterwards my sister Ellen drives me to Northampton where she also lives. July 9 she drops me at Nancy's Clark Street house. I peruse the rooms looking for what's new or missing, check refrigerator for this year's postcards and cartoons. Put my stuff in the upstairs guest room.

Then we're off into it! Caught and caught again. Next time we look up, it's 9:00 pm. We open the French wine (toujours rouge), make salad and rice and veggies. All good.

Norah Zuniga Shaw has come on board as consulting editor, beautifully organizing Nancy's Life Stories into short sections and entitling each. We needed this. Dave Snider, our graphics colleague, has the entire book on his computer awaiting final decisions. During the next five days he and we redesign front and back covers, change and re-change the Q & A column widths, settle on several fonts and leadings, shuffle new images, twice send the entire book from Eugene to satellite to Northampton. Amazing!

By now some of our original choices for photos seem passé. We add several more current ones, lightly shifting the balance and harmony. The proper shape and dimension of the Talk Bubble has slowed us up. Dave S suggests an alternative—like a Polaroid snapshot with a personal letter. We like the look. The last two days are spent in Mike's studio once again laying out every page in order, taping on new scanned images, letting go of several, reevaluating the entire work. Balance and harmony.

July 14. Time for me to catch my train back to NYC. But first we must make two hard copies of the latest *Caught by Surprise*. And it's done. Sister Ellen scoops me up and drives to Springfield train station. I find a seat with a table, thinking to go through the entire book, make some notes, while it's all still fresh. But what really happens is I fall asleep.

7/31/07 Home stretch-er

Time to review just how far (not ask why) we've come. Since 1994 when the clouds opened and a mischievous sweet-smiling Angel whispered to me, "Nancy Stark Smith is waiting to hear from you." And in several winks of an eye—voila!—our book, yet untitled, approaches printing.

Our vision of the book has grown, shrunk, shape-shifted...and, as with other decade-plus projects, found an existence independent of our respective lives. A mostly legitimate offspring. Conceived in love—for my own life, for Nancy, for this mystical, mundane game: Contact Improvisation.

July 12–15, 2007, I was invited to perform at Oregon Country Fair; as well, the scheduled book retreat in which Nancy and Norah Zuniga Shaw—bless her—were to come to terms with all the major texts, finalize format, and send them here for me to agree or object to.

And, with necessary quantum ado, that's just what happened. We added several new photos of Nancy's mother, Lucy; altered the Talk Bubble graphic; Life Stories got titles; Q & A had their numbers removed; Table of contents was agreed upon; the windshield was simplified; The Underscore came to peace; and **1 more angel**, none other than Nancy herself, was added.

photo: Tinu Hettich

Nancy letting her hair down (and up) during a 90-second solo at the end of her January 2007 workshop, Smith College Crew House, Northampton, MA.

Completion is no juried competition.

Nancy has justly argued that when our book is finished, what will then provide us impetus to communicate? True that. Then again we can't really know until that day arrives.

photo: Terra Montgomery

David dressing for *Sphenoid*, Eugene, OR, 1995.

...last call...

Almost since the beginning, say 1996, we called our book-dialogue-project *Caught by Surprise*, or *CBS*, or simply *Caught*. That aspect of CI which is pure pleasure, ebullience in the movement form.

When *Taken by Surprise* (Gere/Albright) appeared in 2003, Nancy and I balked. Sending us into titleless tailspin. Egads!

Since then every e-mail, postcard, telephone call has some or several poignant references to a potentially possible book title: *Gravity's Partner; My Body, My Playmate; Falling into Good Hands; Caught.* And then like cathedral bells on Easter—*Caught Falling*. That's our calling.

CI36 began to loom upon Nancy's horizon—another monumental enterprise. Then, again these seemingly disparate phenomenon could justly converge. Couldn't they?

Which brings us to today—12/15/07—where downstairs, in Fox Hollowland at the table, Nancy and Dave Snider laptop and coffee and chat and snack and gig and wiggle this book toward its rigid state: ready for Jamie the proofreader's keen and discriminating eyes...and the printer.

Each page got finalized. No more changes. As we got into the "back matter," and eventually the vaguely eccentric epi-chrono-logue, the question arose:

how much space will the final one take?

Caught Falling is our celebration of, our offering to, CI, which has continuously nurtured and inspired us. Contact Improvisation is intrinsic to the fabric of the book on each page, in our ongoing dialogue, Nancy and I, our souls' first-choice dance.

David Koteen
2008

photo: Suellen Thomson-Link

DK in *Moulin d'Amour*, Eugene, OR, late 1980s.

biographical notes

DAVID KOTEEN

Born: NYC 2/18/45
Aquarius — Taurus — Taurus
Grades 1-12, Pleasantville, NY
B.A., 1967, Haverford College, Am. Lit.

Initiator: Hearthwind Community, Umpqua, OR
Children of the Green Earth
(UN Tree planting organization)
TApRoOT arts nonprofit
The Wheelbarrow Group (for-profit)

Writings
Novel: *IV Passings To A Bridg-gap*
Short fiction: *Among The Unfertilized Ladies*
Decay's Miscellany
Poetry: *Foreigners' Prayerbook*
Sunday Morning Meditations
Foreigners' Psaltery
Illustrated stories
w/ Tonia Blum: *Red and the Wolf*
w/ C. A. Marlow: *Custard Apples*
Nuff Said
Some Seals
Light Oracles: *Mist Fortune Cards*

Contact Improvisation: since 1981
3 Male Offspring: Ry, Japhet, Azur
CDs: *Climb on Top of Me*
Mistories: The Fool's Gold's Tales

Musical: *HERESY*
Movie: *Again Kiss Again*
Healing Arts: LMT/Polarity Therapy

www.koteen.org

Photo: Bright Crosswell

High School Yearbook

High School Yearbook

photo: Doug Craft

NANCY STARK SMITH

Born: February 11, 1952. Brooklyn, NY
Aquarius — Leo — Scorpio
Raised and schooled: Great Neck, NY
B.A., 1974, Oberlin College, Dance and Writing

Further education:
Tai chi chuan (since 1975, teachers include Jane & Bataan Faigao and Maggie Newman); modern dance (Brenda Way, Betty Lind); postmodern dance (Twyla Tharp, Steve Paxton, Barbara Dilley, and the Grand Union); Body-Mind Centering (Bonnie Bainbridge Cohen and other BMC teachers); ballet barre at the Bates Dance Festival (Jackie Villamil and Rachel List); Tibetan Buddhist meditation (Chögyam Trungpa Rinpoche and others); poetry and book publishing (Diane di Prima/Eidelon Editions)

Co-founder:
Contact Improvisation (1972, with Steve Paxton and others)
Contact Quarterly dance journal (1975)
Contact Collaborations, a 501(c)(3), nonprofit (1978)
Contact Editions, dance book publisher/distributor (1981)

Activity post-college:
Teaching and performing Contact Improvisation and other improvised dance work at schools, art centers, studios, and festivals throughout the U.S. and around the world.
Editing, producing, and publishing *Contact Quarterly* dance journal and other dance literature.
Organizing dance workshops, conferences, events, and other forums for dance practice, research, and exchange.

Continents not reached:
Antarctica

Major events co-produced:
15 years of A Cappella Motion workshop (Northampton, Mass.)
First two years of ECITE (European CI Teachers Exchange), Amsterdam, 1985 & 1986
CI25 (1997) and CI36 (2008) CI anniversary celebrations
Moving's View workshop; NSS January workshop, CITE

Videos/DVDs/films (with NSS):
Fall After Newton; Chute; Contact at 10th and 2nd; Peripheral Vision, by Videoda
The Poetics of Touch: Nancy Stark Smith, a Pathway into Contact Improvisation; a video by Sara Pozzoli, Germana Siciliani, © 2006

Writings:
Editor notes and articles for *Contact Quarterly* since 1975.
Chapters and articles in the following books:
Taken by Surprise, edited by A. Cooper Albright & D. Gere
Contact Improvisation, by Cheryl Pallant
CQ/CI Sourcebook, by *Contact Quarterly*/Contact Editions

Significant dance/performance/magazine collaborators:
Steve Paxton, Danny Lepkoff, Lisa Nelson, Christina Svane, Andrew Harwood, Karen Nelson, Collin Walcott (music), Julyen Hamilton, Kirstie Simson, Simone Forti, Group 6 (Chris Aiken, Peter Bingham, Jeff Bliss, Julie Carr, and Ray Chung, Ruth Zaporah, Lila Hurwitz (Ibirdesign), Mike Vargas (music)–and this book with David Koteen!

Select performance works:
Buddy, Come Home (1983); *Cardboard Caravan, Nameless Warmth* (1984, with Andrew Warshaw); *Dancing in Moving Pictures* (1986, with K. Nelson, A. Alessi, and A. Harwood); *Everything Must Go* (1989, with Karen Nelson); *Raku* (1991-present; solo); *Asterisk* (*) (1999-present, with musician Mike Vargas); *Exactness of Weights of Feeling* (2007, group piece, made in Finland with Mike Vargas); *Baseline* (2004, 2007, with Peter Bingham, Mike Vargas, and James Proudfoot [lights])

www.nancystarksmith.com

photo/image credits

PAGE #, PHOTOGRAPHER/ARTIST

Front cover photo, Uldis Ohaks
All hieroglyphs, Nancy Stark Smith
i, iii, iv, vii, Roger Kose

Prologue

viii, Bruce Newhouse

Introduction

x, Mark Stone

What Is Contact Improvisation?

xi, Stephen Petegorsky
xii, unknown
xiii, Raisa Kyllikki Karjalainen
xiv, Bruce Newhouse
xv, Ted Pushinsky

Views Through the Windshield

pg. 2, left, Esty Stowell
pg. 2, rt, Bill Arnold
pg. 3, unknown
pg. 4, left, JJ Smith (Nancy's father)
pg. 4, rt, *Life* photo: Marie Hansen
pg. 5, JJ Smith
pg. 6, left, unknown
pg. 6, rt, unknown
pg. 7, two above, unknown
pg. 7, below, Bill Arnold
pg. 8, left, JJ Smith
pg. 8, rt, above, JJ Smith
pg. 8, rt, below, unknown
pg. 9, above, JJ Smith
pg. 9, below, JJ Smith
pg. 10, unknown
pg. 11, left, JJ Smith
pg. 11, rt, JJ Smith
pg. 12, left, unknown
pg. 12, rt, JJ Smith
pg. 13, above, JJ Smith
pg. 13, below, JJ Smith
pg. 14, above, JJ Smith
pg. 14, below, Steve Rattner
pg. 15, Ted Pushinsky
pg. 16, Bill Arnold
pg. 17, Chris Harris
pg. 18, left, Bill Arnold
pg. 18, rt, Bill Arnold
pg. 19, Doug Winter
pg. 20, above, Heidi Timm
pg. 20, below, Bill Arnold
pg. 21, unknown
pg. 22, painting by Polly Thompson
pg. 23, left, Bill Arnold
pg. 23, rt, unknown
pg. 24, left, Ruth E. Carsch
pg. 24, rt, Bill Arnold
pg. 25, left (flyer), NSS & Steve Paxton
pg. 25, rt, Uldis Ohaks
pg. 26, Bill Arnold
pg. 27, Uldis Ohaks
pg. 28, David Minehart
pg. 29, Bill Arnold
pg. 30, unknown
pg. 31, Bill Arnold
pg. 32, Edmund Shea
pg. 33, Bill Arnold
pg. 34, Bill Arnold
pg. 35, Stephen Petegorsky
pg. 36, Larry Myers
pg. 37, left, drawing by Susan Schell
pg. 37, rt, Bill Arnold
pg. 38, Rhoda Mae Evans
pg. 39, Chris Harris
pg. 40, above, Bill Arnold
pg. 40, below, Robert Tobey
pg. 41, Marianne Pappas
pg. 42, Bill Arnold
pg. 43, drawings by Susan Schell
pg. 44, Bill Arnold
pg. 45, Bill Arnold
pg. 46, Ted Pushinsky
pg. 47, drawing by Susan Schell; program/puzzle by Karen Nelson, NSS
pg. 48, Bill Arnold
pg. 49, Lou Stewart Danielson
pg. 50, above, Bill Arnold
pg. 50, below, JJ Smith
pg. 51, Uldis Ohaks
pg. 52, Alix King
pg. 53, above, left, unknown

pg. 53, above, rt, Bob Mann
pg. 53, below, unknown
pg. 54, Bill Arnold
pg. 55, Gil Grossi
pg. 56, watercolor by Lisa Leizman
pg. 57, Bill Arnold
pg. 58, Serge Gubelman
pg. 59, above, Ray Chung
pg. 59, below, left, Ray Chung
pg. 59, below, rt, Ray Chung
pg. 60, Emma Dodge Hanson
pg. 61, TAP participant
pg. 62, Bill Arnold
pg. 63, Steve Paxton
pg. 64, drawings, Susan Schell
pg. 65, left, Bill Arnold
pg. 65, above, rt, Ray Chung
pg. 65, below, rt, Ray Chung
pg. 66, Bill Arnold
pg. 67, Bill Arnold
pg. 68, Bill Arnold
pg. 69, Bill Arnold
pg. 70, Leonie Ravestein
pg. 71, Lisa Nelson
pg. 72, Ray Chung
pg. 73, above, NSS
pg. 73, below, NSS
pg. 74, still from video by Jennifer Kayle
pg. 75, left, NSS
pg. 75, rt, drawing by Mike Vargas
pg. 76, Bill Arnold
pg. 77, drawing by Mike Vargas
pg. 78, left, *Life* photo: Marie Hansen
pg. 78, rt, photo & cover design unknown
pg. 79, Bill Arnold
pg. 81, left, score by NSS
pg. 81, rt, Chris Randle
pg. 82, Tinu Hettich
pg. 83, Bill Arnold
pg. 84, above, JJ Smith
pg. 84, below, NSS

Backwords

pg. 86, NSS
pg. 87, Uldis Ohaks
pg. 88, Ted Pushinsky
pg. 89, Uldis Ohaks

The Underscore

pg. 90, drawing by NSS
pg. 91, left, NSS
pgs. 91–96, Underscore symbols, NSS
pg. 93, Raisa Kyllikki Karjalainen
pg. 96, NSS
pg. 97, NSS
pg. 98, Barbara Stahlberger
pg. 99, left, map by NSS
pg. 99, rt, *Proximity* cover photo by Catherine Magill

Epi-Chrono-Logue

pg. 100, Bruce Newhouse
pg. 102, Terra Montgomery
pg. 103, NSS
pg. 104, unknown origin
pg. 105, left, Tinu Hettich
pg. 105, rt, Terra Montgomery
pg. 106, Suellen Thomson-Link

Biographical Notes

pg. 107, [DK] top, Bright Crosswell
pg. 107, high school yearbook photos
pg. 107, [NSS] bottom, Doug Craft

Photo/Image Credits

pg. 109, photogram, Bill Arnold

Last page

pg. 112, NSS

Photogram by Bill Arnold

Birthday Poem, by Christina Svane
February 11, 1994

*
* *
* * *
* * * *

so happy birthday
in the uselessness of columbine
climbing crazily purple on your porch

happy birthday
in the wasted hours of wandering
up the woods-path to the mandala

happy birthday
in the senselessness of scribbling
dreams no-one but you will ever read

on the day
you and your mother
did this, you were happy

in the duet
she danced with you
great happiness is preserved

in the happiness
of finding a mother and a path
questions of usefulness dissolve like snow on the tongue

long is the great grey braid
that has accompanied you through the years
famous in its own right, like a hero's horse

long is the list of the people you have taught
and have learned well enough
to teach in their turn

long is the lineage you carry with you
unknown, unnamed, undaunted
by the leap required to speak

from across centuries
across cultures
and continents.

I gave you no choice
but to let me come with you
north up the coast in 'seventy six

one night you had a vision
through the poet's magic methods
that spelled out your purpose in this life

in the sanctuary of the cab of your camper
with the lights of the harbor glowing behind you in the night
like birthday candles waiting for you to make your wish

you confided not in me, I felt, but the night
that you had been chosen to be a teacher
and the word stretched out ahead of us like the road

* * * *
* * *
* *
*

*
* *
* * *
* * * *

you followed that road for twenty years
and it has brought you home
to a home that is really yours

so happy housewarming
may the hole you cut in the ceiling
warm your bedroom above

may the living room marry the kitchen
and give birth to a new sense of space
just as you envision it

may the rabbits get the message
that you're serious about your garden
and you're not going anywhere soon

and may all the unexpected things
that arise when one truly feels at home
'Greatness,' Goethe calls it, arise for you

right where you are
in the shade of a maple
at the edge of town

near the top of a hill
with the woods in your shadow
and the ferns at your feet

a chest full of presents
your mother left for you
has been waiting for this moment

fragile things and heavy things
that do not travel well
but need walls to hang and lean against, windows to gaze out of

mysterious pictures in fantasy frames
mirrors that seem to be doorways
crystal, miraculously in tact

happy unpacking
I hear tissue crackling
and see peach-colored silk in your hands

a small leather-bound book
with gilt lettering
and her inscription

I am very quiet beside you
I should almost not be here, it seems
but that is how close we are, that it is alright

it begins to snow as it gets dark
like tiny white pieces of paper
filling the sky with messages that will never be read

mandalas, poems, mosaics
symmetries, crystalline jewels
birthday blessings from the bardo of existence

* * * *
* * *
* *
*

*
* *
* * *
* * * *

for your birthday
I would have taken you
to see Little Buddha
which starts and ends in Bhutan
this barley paper
is also from Bhutan
it has a small story

Justine took me to my first modern dance class
barefoot we crossed the Victorian floor
imaging eggshells not to be broken

three children later, all boys,
she moved from the mountains of Switzerland
to the mountains of Bhutan, staying four years

her man was a forester
sent to help them preserve their forests
but he also helped them preserve their monasteries

rebuilding roofs
and purchasing piles of paper
the last old monk who knew how, made all day

day after day one by one
sheet by sheet he stacked them up
happily filling room after room with the paper he made

it did not matter
that nobody bought it
besides Justine's husband

he did not make it
to supply a demand
but to keep the knowledge of how to make it alive

when Justine and her family moved to Africa
she gave me a stack of this paper, rolled up
and said, Here, this is for your poetry

and now I think I should try to be
like that old paper-maker
happily filling rooms with poem after poem day after day

someone swung the pendulum
and hypnotized us into thinking
we must make ourselves useful

that is the spell
this paper
breaks.

* * * *
* * *
* *
*